Affirm press

Lennox Nicholson arrived at the end of his twenties with a desk full of unfinished stories, synopses, screenplays and a severe drinking and drug problem. Sobering up, he completed a Bachelor of Writing & Publishing at NMIT and an internship with Affirm Press. He lives in Melbourne, with no pets, no kids and no hangovers. *On the Wagon* is his first book.

On the Wagon

LENNOX NICHOLSON

To Hank Richelieu,

the finest writer/limo driver/community farmer in New Orleans, maybe the world. Thanks for your hospitality and help in making this book happen.

Len.

AFFIRM press

Published by Affirm Press in 2017
28 Thistlethwaite Street, South Melbourne, VIC 3205.
www.affirmpress.com.au
10 9 8 7 6 5 4 3 2 1

Text and copyright © Lennox Nicholson
All rights reserved. No part of this publication may be reproduced without prior permission of the publisher.

National Library of Australia Cataloguing-in-Publication entry available for this title.

Title: On the Wagon / Lennox Nicholson, author.
ISBN: 9781925344578 (paperback)

Cover design by Karen Wallis
Interior photographs by Jimmy Delane
Typeset in 12/20 Garamond Premier Pro by J&M Typesetting
Proudly printed in Australia by Griffin Press

The paper this book is printed on is certified against the Forest Stewardship Council® Standards. Griffin Press holds FSC chain of custody certification SGS-COC-005088. FSC promotes environmentally responsible, socially beneficial and economically viable management of the world's forests.

'He and I suddenly saw the whole country like an oyster for us to open,' Sal says, 'and the pearl was there, the pearl was there.'

Chapter One

I'd been out until 8am on New Year's Day, and hadn't had even a sip of alcohol. I had held firm although everyone around me had been enthusiastically imbibing the spirit of the occasion. What a legend.

New Year's Day was a hot one, 30-something degrees with that north wind whipping through Melbourne from the great deserts of Central Australia. I felt sorry for all the people nursing hangovers. It was a day when a sophisticated drinker – someone like me, for example, who hadn't got messed up the night before – might have a gin and tonic and quench their thirst. Yes. One. In a tall glass. With a slice of lemon. So I dropped by the bottle shop and bought myself a one-litre bottle of gin, a couple of bottles of tonic water and a handful of lemons.

I remember reading the label on the back of the empty bottle later that night to see how many standard drinks it contained, and thinking that if one person put away that many standard drinks they should be well and truly drunk, if not unconscious. But I was still steady enough to get the scotch and cask wine from the cupboard.

I explained this to the triage nurse at the Emergency Department the next day. I've been here before, I said, I know what I'm doing. I had drunk so much, again, that I was sure I was going to have a seizure – again. So if it was okay with her, I'd just sit in the Emergency Department with my book waiting to have said seizure. I'd rather it happen in the safety of the hospital than at home alone where I could get injured because, well, that would be irresponsible.

She cocked her head gently to one side and asked, 'Mr Nicholson, have you ever thought about quitting drinking?'

'Yeah, I have,' I said. 'I went to an AA meeting once.'

'Have you thought about going back?'

An invisible hand slapped me across the face. Hard. Then it slapped me again. 'Um, I haven't. I think I might though.'

As I left the hospital, I thumbed through my wallet looking for a business card I vaguely remembered putting there some weeks ago, given to me by a man at the Alcoholics

Anonymous meeting. I had sat there without saying a word, and he'd leaned over to me and said, 'Listen mate, no one can tell you you're an alcoholic or not, it's something you need to decide for yourself.' He looked me up and down, and said, 'But I think you are.' It was kind of a funny moment and as I took the card he held out to me, I thought to myself, *get fucked*.

But now I called him and he sounded like he'd been expecting me and that it was no big deal, this stranger telephoning out of the blue. Among other things, he told me where there was a meeting that night. I still had a car and – somehow – my driver's licence, so I drove down to where the meeting was held. I sat in the car with the engine running, watching people enter the building. I could drive off if I felt like it. No one would know.

In the years preceding my enlightening discussion with that triage nurse, I'd ploughed through jobs, relationships, housing situations, opportunities, friendships, you name it, the whole time thinking this kind of living would surely, eventually, give me insight into the human condition – enough so I could write down something meaningful.

I was 29 and this was my 'career path'. I'd 'retired' from everything else; that's how it felt and that's what I told people. In reality, I smoked so much weed I couldn't learn anything anymore, like how to use the new touchscreen cash register the pub I'd been working in had installed, so for that and a few other reasons, I was asked to leave. Without that regular income, I resorted to withdrawing cash advances from credit cards to pay my rent and bills and to have money for booze and drugs, plus my latest shitbox car. It only took three months to get $20,000 into debt.

It was all part of that bigger plan, though: the tortured existence that would give me unique insight. I would write a book about bypassing the daily grind, describing how I did just that and made a living from the royalties. It made perfect sense but only I could see it, because only I had the clarity and the freedom that came from shutting off to everything else.

But I couldn't write. Ten years working behind a bar meant I hadn't experienced quite enough of life outside of strip clubs and pubs. I used to turn on the computer, open a bottle of wine and ruminate on the work that lay in front of me. Drink, type a few lines, repeat. By the end of a couple of paragraphs, I'd begin rehearsing acceptance speeches in my head. Drink, rehearse, repeat. I wasn't one of those drunken writers who churned out 100 per cent shit either. It was only about 99.99 per cent shit. And I never, ever finished anything. Soon enough, I skipped the writing part altogether.

Drink, repeat.

Lacking that motivation to get the words down, I slept in until four in the afternoon, smoked weed for breakfast and devoured casks of red wine and cheap scotch until I passed out again. The guy I was sharing the flat with would check to see if I was still alive when he left for work in the morning. Seeing as I was face down on the carpet in front of the door, it would have been rude of him not to at least look for a pulse. When he kindly woke me, I'd drag myself the few metres to my room and crawl into bed.

This was freedom. No big plans any more, no potential, no telling myself I wouldn't do it tomorrow. No job, no relationship, no mark on the world. I just emerged every day at whatever time, rolled a joint and started drinking as soon as it seemed the right thing to do, which was always sooner rather than later.

But there was also a niggling part of me that thought this was also how people ended up homeless and dead in the gutter. I knew I had to drown out that sick fucking logic before it destroyed me, quiet it just long enough to get the breakthrough I knew was coming for me as a writer. It made sense that it was going to be harder the closer I got to breaking through.

I wasn't born 29 years old passed out on the living room floor but I was scared I might be dead before my thirtieth birthday. With me left in charge, my life had become unmanageable.

•

That's where my life was when I turned off the car engine and walked into that AA meeting, into a room full of people who wouldn't normally mix. Men, women, old, young, bums, suits. I took a seat and listened to a woman talk about how she hadn't had a drink for six years. Six years? Why was she still coming? I listened to another guy and thought, *Jesus, I'm glad I'm not as fucked up as he is*. Then the guy in the chair at the front pointed and said, 'You in the red T-shirt, would you like to share?'

Lucky for me I didn't know that you can just say no if you don't want to. I copied the others and told a room full of strangers what I'd been up to. How I'd woken in fright inside my car not knowing where I was, so I'd tried to drive home in a panic, hit something and shredded the rubber off the tyres. I'd abandoned the car and bought another one on credit. I told them about my 'retirement' and how I'd stopped telling myself I wouldn't drink tonight. I told them that I was at the point where I couldn't drink and I couldn't not drink any more. And they applauded me, which felt completely weird. It was only later that I realised they were congratulating me on telling myself the truth, not them. It was devastating, because I'd resisted it for so long, but also incredibly liberating.

I asked if there was someone my age I could talk to, and got introduced to Mitch, who had been sober just under a year. The only thing I remember him telling me that night was to just keep coming back to meetings.

I returned the next night, and met another guy in his twenties named Shane. He looked like he'd just walked out of a Gillette commercial but he assured me he was in a hell of a state between the ears. I remember him telling me that sometimes not drinking comes down to a minute at a time, not just a day at a time. Driving home, I thought about pulling into the drive-through bottle shop near my house when I heard Shane's voice in my head: 'A minute at a time.' I wondered if he'd meant that driving past instead of driving in was not drinking one minute at a time.

It was only when I got home that night that I realised I'd drunk everything in the house. There was nothing left. So I went to bed without a drink. The next day it occurred to me that I hadn't drunk anything the day or night before. A day at a time. Those people in AA knew something I didn't. I wanted to know more of what they knew, to learn how they did this thing. They'd got their lives back and kept them. I wanted what they had.

Alcoholics Anonymous isn't about self-help: it's a program based on helping others, which made no sense to me at first. The culture is about putting alcohol down, not picking it back up again and, most importantly, taking personal responsibility. Step One laid it all out on the table: We were powerless over alcohol and our lives had become unmanageable. The gift in the meetings, or 'the rooms' as they are commonly known, is desperation.

I kept going to meetings and kept not drinking. At first I thought AA was just about stopping drinking but I slowly realised that it's mostly about devoting yourself to living life without needing to start again. Through going to the meetings, I began to see my life clearly. It wasn't pretty, but nor was it without hope. Minutes became days became years and still I wasn't drinking. I talked regularly at the meetings and people applauded; strangers talked and we applauded them too. Reminding ourselves of that moment we realised we were beat was a powerful thing: to not dwell on it in a sad-sack kind of way, but to never forget where we don't want to return.

I went to a good school and my parents are still married after more than 50 years. I was never abused, my childhood was great, I had family and friends and although we weren't rich, we never suffered either. Thing is, I'm an alcoholic, a junkie for instant gratification. I innately crave a sense of ease and comfort. I have personal default settings of restlessness, irritability and a general feeling of discontent. I discovered that alcohol alleviates these feelings. I also discovered that once I had a drink, there was no off switch, but it took a long time before that mattered to me. Once I got a taste for getting that sense of ease and comfort immediately, I made all my decisions based on having that as the outcome and found other people who did it that way too. Left in charge, that's the best I could manage. It's nobody's fault, just the hand I've been dealt, the way I'm wired. Like having type 1 diabetes: I simply acquired a condition that, if left unchecked, would be lethal, but the symptoms can be arrested with certain daily practices.

Over the years, I'd tried to help myself. I'd changed jobs from casual bar work to more professional roles in the hope that having to be there at a certain time and behave a certain way would curb my drinking. It didn't. I left relationships and started new ones with people I thought were totally different, but I inevitably drank the same and the relationships deteriorated in the same way. I'd talked to shrinks, lied to specialists and read books on self-improvement. I could even stop on my own too, especially during an 'alcohol-free week', which generally lasted about four or five days. I didn't go to a rehab or do a detox. I didn't know what those were and I didn't have any money or health insurance. So I ended up going to AA.

So there I was – in my early thirties, not drinking, attending AA, and trying to grow up. The challenge was that, apart from trying to deal with an addiction, I was still a teenager in many ways, especially emotionally, my growth stunted at the point where drinking became my life's main focus. I was a sort of grotesque man-child, barely equipped for life, falling short of the expectations others might have of me. In the AA rooms, they understood, and I got comfort there. No temples, no mountain tops, no ocean crossings. Just meetings. It's not even close to a cult either. No cult I've ever heard of tells its members to go back to work, participate in the community and rebuild relations with their family and friends.

AA's Big Book defines alcoholism as a mental obsession and a physical allergy: alcoholism involves a reaction to your first drink that means not being able to stop having more until something else intervenes, like passing out. Or handcuffs. Or your heart no longer beating. That's what it was like for me when I wasn't drinking – if I wasn't thinking about when and where I'd be drinking again, I'd be thinking about the drinking I'd just done. Obsession isn't always a bad thing. If you're obsessed with living a balanced life and helping others, the results will probably be pretty good. If you're a professional athlete looking to win, obsession is a prerequisite. But having a persistent recurring compulsion to use a substance or engage in a specific behaviour that will have harmful consequences to your health, mental state or social life, well, that's obsession turned nightmare.

These guys believe that the alcoholic needs to be free from the bondage of self while also realising that the thought of picking up a drink is an unconquerable obsession. Whatever is going on out there is almost irrelevant – it's what's going on inside that's doing the damage. I really got into this idea of freedom from the bondage of self: selfishness, dishonesty, fear, pride, resentment, self-pity, intolerance; all the stuff of the human experience, which gets amplified tenfold for an alcoholic. All the stuff I thought I was mining for insight as a writer while life was happening around (or stepping over) me.

AA helped me but it wasn't a cure, and never will be. It doesn't work like that. My steering is still a bit wonky, and if it's not constantly monitored, it'll run me off the road.

•

After I had been going to meetings for a few years, my life had done a U-turn. I'd held the same job and even enrolled in a writing course at university. But I still had youthful impulses and an insatiable want for a full life. I was also concerned that I was tethered to the support of the meetings. Could I cope free range? Or had I just replaced one addiction with another? (Albeit a much healthier one where I'm more liable to bore my loved ones to death than sweep them up in my deluded destruction.)

Onto that fertile ground blew a seed: a movie trailer for *On the Road*. 'A young writer trying to take off,' said the voiceover. '"The only people that interest me are the mad ones, the ones that are mad to live, mad to talk, desirous of everything at the same time. The ones that never yawn or say a commonplace thing but burn, burn, burn like roman candles across the night."'

Yes! That was me, and I was hooked!

I set out to read the novel before watching the film, as I often claim that the movie can be better than the book, even though the irony is not lost on me that I, supposedly an aspiring writer, had not thought to read this classic sooner. But I couldn't read everything – it would have encroached on all my drinking time.

I read about Sal Paradise living in New York and meeting Dean Moriarty, the side-burned hero from the snowy west who lights a fire under Sal's arse and gets him on the road to Denver and beyond. I raced through page after page, reading about guys with names like Remi Boncoeur and Bull Lee and Carlo Marx, all poets and writers and thinkers, put down on paper by Jack Kerouac, the book's real Sal Paradise, the best writer of the lot. There's hitching a ride on a flat-bed truck, passing a bottle around with other travellers on their way through the middle of America; there's hitting on pretty girls in Des Moines, and writing love notes on the back of dollar bills for Mexican waitresses in Cheyenne, and Rita waiting for Sal in Denver. The 'kicks' and the camaraderie and the ideas and the conversations and how great it is to have only a few dollars in your pocket but all the freedom in the world; all you need is some good friends, a car, a girl and a bottle of whiskey.

That's how I would have read the book at 19. But now I was reading the story about Sal and Dean's life on the road with drunk experience and sober eyes, and it gave me an uneasy feeling. I read about the frantic movement, the desperation, the longing. The cars, the girls, the kicks, all of it. I could feel that longing, that need to get away from anywhere to feel better, but I could also see the fundamental flaw in the plan. Jack Kerouac, our Sal Paradise in the novel, and Neal Cassady, *On the Road's* Dean Moriarty, drove all over the States for years, searching for the solution to their restlessness and discontent. But maybe the reason they never found it 'out there' was because they never realised the problems were 'inside' – the demons in their heads. Maybe the real problem was that they always took themselves along for the ride.

Or maybe they just didn't find any pearl of wisdom that would explain their discontent and powerlessness over their own impulses; maybe they drove straight past it and missed the damn thing. Was the obsessive, abusive behaviour of an addict really what drove Sal and Dean across the country in the name of freedom? Is an answer out there, I wondered, on the routes they took in their mad dashes across the country back and forth and back and forth, holding out hope of finding some kind of freedom right up until the bitter end?

The applied wisdom I was hearing in all the AA meetings was great, but is the mundane attendance, week in and week out, really all there is to this freedom business? Doesn't it need to be put to the test in a world that puts alcoholics in early graves to really prove its worth? Deep within me grew a desire to look for myself and to find out if Kerouac and I were seeking the same thing. Is freedom 'out there', or do I really need to just keep coming back to AA? Are their principles something I can take with me and use to ensure I'm free from picking up a drink but also free to roam as I please through the world? What even is freedom? Is it a tangible thing or a way of living your life? Or is it, like Nina Simone said, just a feeling? Is freedom only the indulgence of obsessions and dependence, or is it the release from their grip? Perhaps, if you want to be well on all fronts, you have to do what it takes, wherever you are; you must remain vigilant over yourself as much as others to keep that freedom feeling.

Surely there was more to this idea. I'd have to find out from people in all the places Sal and Dean passed through. Could I take my brand of freedom with me or would I discover it was all hanging by a thread from a comfortable bubble of local AA meetings and familiarity? If Sal couldn't find freedom on the road, would I be able to even keep mine?

Kerouac was 25 when he began the first journey in *On the Road*. When I was 25, my greatest achievement was a house party where most of the bottles and cans ended up in the recycling bin. At 29, when Kerouac wrote the 'scroll draft', I was walking into my first AA meeting, sure that if I didn't quit drinking immediately I'd die before hitting 30. Kerouac was 35 when *On the Road* was published, the same age I was when I first read the book and saw the gleaming traits of active alcoholism I'd been learning about for the last few years. By 47, he was dead.

•

One Wednesday night I'm at a local meeting, early, making myself a cup of tea in the kitchen. Jimmy Delane, a photographer friend of mine and fellow member, sidles up to the bench.

'Lenny. What have you been up to?' he says.

'Well actually I've booked a ticket to fly to the US. I'm going to cross overland from New York to San Francisco. I'm following the route from Jack Kerouac's *On the Road* and then going to end up at that massive AA convention in Atlanta, at the meeting to beat all meetings.'

Jimmy leans against a table in the centre of the kitchen,

arms folded, looking at the floor. He had clearly been expecting less from his enquiry. Then he looks up.

'Wait, you're doing a road trip across the US?'

'Yeah.'

'When?'

'I fly out in June.'

'How long for?'

'About six weeks.'

His eyes widen. It's like a light is growing inside of him. 'Who are you going with?'

'Anyone who wants in. You want in, you're in. Just fly over and get in the car.'

'Are you taking the missus?'

'Nah, Annie can't get the time off work. Just me at the moment.'

'I'm coming.'

'Well, best you book a flight then,' I say.

For the entire meeting, Jimmy has that look of someone who's received news of something almost unbelievable yet completely simple and probable. I know he's imagining the photographs he will take, the great portraits he'll capture. After the meeting, he comes over to double-check that I hadn't made the whole thing up.

'Yes, road trip,' I say. 'USA, June.'

Even though I rarely saw him outside of meetings, Jimmy was the right man at the right time to join me for this trip. He always seemed to be wearing a white T-shirt and trousers, like he'd been waiting in the late-40s Beat uniform Kerouac always wore in anticipation of a call-up.

At the time, I took the fact that my travelling companion was a skilled photographer who had always wanted to do a US road trip and had just given himself three months off from his business without making plans as a sure sign that this project was destined. Jimmy made the decision to join me for the New York to LA leg of the trip with relish, but he had to get his head around my plan, which was to have no real plan beyond a list of places I wanted to visit. I would make no arrangements save for telling a few people who knew people who knew people where we would probably be going and when, namely a man named Tim Ulrich who, my sponsor assured me, knew people. But that's it. It wouldn't be following the Beat path if it all went silky smooth with great organisation. For the logistics, I would put the call out to the universe and put myself – and Jimmy – at the mercy of the network of strangers we might meet through the fellowship of AA. I wanted to experience our own sort of recklessness and see what it kicked up.

Chapter Two

Touching down at JFK airport, I'm in the middle of that long-flight twilight zone; that feeling where I know I'm not home but I'm not quite sure where I've arrived either. Getting into the US is strangely easy considering my passport photo looks like I've been up for three days on a bender and didn't shower before getting it taken, because that's exactly what happened: gaunt face, eyes red and puffy, and I've got that emotionless expression like an Eastern Bloc mug shot from the 80s.

Jimmy and I collect our bags from the carousel, and meander out of the concourse and into the retro oranges and browns and shiny poles of a New York subway carriage. Stepping onto this train is like walking into countless movie scenes embedded in my memory. I do my best not to look completely in awe of being another passenger on a regular New York subway carriage.

We get out near Murray Street, not far from where two planes hit the Twin Towers. I remember watching the reports on TV when it happened. I'd gotten home after working in the bar and was lying on the couch, drinking a beer to wind down. It was three in the morning and one of my housemates had just got home from a night out as the news report about a plane flying into a tower in New York was playing for the first time. As we discussed the event, a second plane hit the other tower. We were confused as to what we were watching and what was happening. When the buildings collapsed, it looked like footage of an intentional demolition, the towers imploding and crumbling in an enormous dust cloud. It was on TV every day from then on for longer than I can remember, and it was labelled an attack on freedom – followed by a war to protect that freedom, which is still going. Jimmy and I pass two armed soldiers quietly standing sentry as we go up the stairs. What's freedom anyway?

On the Manhattan street there are yellow cabs and tall buildings and a cloud of steam. Fucking New York City steam! Coming up from a manhole in the street! My head is spinning while Jimmy is straight onto navigating us toward a Starbucks, which, before I can put up a fight, he assures me is good here. I'm through the door with promise of free wifi. Some time ago, Jimmy quit drinking coffee and swapped it for tea, so he doesn't turn his nose up at this place like I do. But I am happy just to walk a New York City street complete with steam and manholes with 'The Edison Company' imprinted in the metal. I'm in Sal's New York, the starting point of the journey in *On the Road*.

Inside the café there's a table of middle-aged block-party veterans in caps and baggy jeans talking over the top of MacBooks. People flit about outside the window; the crowd is sparse, but it's a Sunday night. Jimmy brings two cardboard cauldrons, teabags dangling over the sides, to the table before getting to work on how to get to the Airbnb apartment he booked us into. I'm not travelling with a strung-out, Benzo-eating madman who stole a car to get us to Jersey like Sal did; I'm travelling with a guy who agonised for weeks over a place to stay, like only an obsessive sober alcoholic would. If you need to get something done, give it to a sober alcoholic in recovery.

Seems we're only a few subway stops from Grove Street in Jersey City, and our accommodation is around the corner from there. Shit, we've been in New York for a half-hour and we're leaving already. I'm glad I didn't get obsessed with every travel detail in *On the Road* and pull the whip out on myself to replicate Sal's footsteps. If I had, I'd be dragging Jimmy on a rain-soaked journey north of New York to Bear Mountain just to turn around and come back again to head west like Sal wanted to in the first place. There's no need for a symbolic false start here; Jimmy and I both had our false start years back before we got sober and we're free to not have to do that again.

I notice Jimmy is barely carrying anything and ask him if he's got enough clothing for three weeks. He assures me he'll just buy everything he needs for the rest of the trip as we go. We get off the subway at Grove Street and come out into a lively square in the middle of Jersey City. Jimmy's digital map leads us straight there. I'm eager to dump the backpack, and Jimmy's keen to verify his selection on Airbnb.

Sal was living in Paterson, New Jersey, with his aunt when Dean Moriarty showed up asking Sal to teach him how to write. He'd had a fight with Marylou in their Hoboken apartment and she'd called the cops, so he took the first of many flights in *On the Road*, this one under the guise of wanting Sal to pass on his literary skills. Sal writes that his aunt calls Dean a madman on sight.

There's no ruse required for Jimmy and me to rent this place; in fact, it's ridiculously easy to get somewhere good to stay these days, lining it up from another country with a few mouse clicks without ever having to have met the owner. Back in my drinking days I would have been too paranoid for this, or just too fearful, to take such a service on face value. We take a lift to a deluxe pad far beyond what I'd expected, and I realise it's too late to ask Jimmy how much it cost. I'd forgotten I was planning to spend as little as possible because I just didn't have money to spend, not out of any shrewd budgeting. There's a huge lounge with a fold-out couch and big screen TV that I have no intention of watching but is comforting to Jimmy. There's also a computer desk laid out in one corner and I naively assume I'll punch a couple of thousand words out each day. Jimmy takes the bedroom, which also has a big screen TV. We head out for a bite but the plane trip and the jet lag and the anticipation catches up and knocks us both on our arses halfway through the meal.

I wake at 6am to the sound of *The Simpsons* blasting from the giant TV in Jimmy's room. He can't work out how to turn the sound down so he just leaves it. I go for a walk to take in the area, stepping out past Jersey workers in denim, hoodies and hard hats ambling onto a big site opposite where we're staying. A few minutes later I'm surrounded by classic split-level terraces, three level rows of crimson apartments, running down the street. Sets of concrete stairs lead to front doors and basements in the style seen in many American TV shows and movies.

A big, beautiful, shiny Jersey fire engine is parked by the kerb, 'Always With Us – 9/11/01' and the names of several deceased firefighters inscribed on its side. Nobody's memory of that event will diminish any time soon, whether they were in New York or watching it on TV. A car next to the truck has an enormous advertisement for the Jersey City public library emblazoned on the hood, with the slogan 'Knowledge for free'. That's what I'm looking for here, knowledge for free. Well, the knowledge is free, but getting here and crossing the country to gain it costs a little money. Especially staying in luxurious pads like the one we're currently in. Can't just jump on a boxcar or steal a car like Dean Moriarty might have, not these days. The subway entrances are guarded by those military sentries and there are plenty of people in American jails for car theft. It's a free country, sure, but I wouldn't want to mess up here in the slightest. Dean Moriarty would never get out of jail in this era.

It suddenly dawns on me how far away I am from my regular routine, the safety and familiarity of people in the AA meetings. I remember an old timer named Gelignite Jack who used to say 'AA is portable', meaning it's not the meetings you regularly go to that keep you sober, it's what you take away from them and put into your daily life. And that's something I've got to face – I won't be able to live much of a life if I'm on a knife-edge of sobriety and liable to crack if I don't have regular meetings. That's definitely not freedom.

But Gelignite also used to say, 'We're playing for high stakes – we're playing for our lives.' I've seen people decide they've got this thing licked and move far away or overseas and stop doing what they used to do to stay sober. Most get a scare and then get back to working their twelve-step program. Some drink and lose a couple of months or years and tell the tale at meetings. An old friend of mine named Nico did that a couple of times, moving from the east coast to the west coast of Australia and back, before the last move left him with no one around and nothing to do, and his last drink left him dead on the end of a needle.

I get back to the pad and Jimmy is keen for his morning bagel and tea. He's almost salivating at the prospect of going to this local bagel joint his girlfriend recommended. White T-shirts and food – the wheelhouse of this guy's travels. I feel like an adult of some kind after my morning walk; eight years ago I'd have been hungover right now, assuming that, if I'd kept on drinking, I'd have even gotten this far out of my suburb.

Jimmy locates this famed bagel store and is giddy with excitement. It surely can't be this lump of dough, I think, as I bite into my bagel; it has to be the surroundings. Jimmy tells me this is the dream part of his day, when he feels inspired and hopeful. And consumes lumps of doughy white bread full of egg and bacon with half a gallon of tea. He's happy that this can be enough these days, rather than being stuck with a constant feeling of wanting more. Sitting at the counter is a guy dressed in work pants, boots and an orange T-shirt with a skull and crossbones logo. 'Union Forever' sits under the design. It turns out he's just been put off from a job. He's from Hoboken, just north of where we're staying, where Dean and Marylou were shacked up. He's very keen to impress on us that we'd love Hoboken if we went there.

But we're here for only two more nights before we head west. I won't be travelling to Kerouac's birthplace in Lowell on any kind of pilgrimage, either. I'd like to, but I don't have six years to cover four cross-country road trips like he did. I've got five weeks to cover as much ground as I can before getting to the massive AA convention in Atlanta. I'm hoping I'll meet someone there – or at least hear someone – who will deliver some gold, some of that stuff I used to hear in what seemed like every meeting I went to in early recovery, before I got busy with all the good things sobriety afforded and forgot about doing the things that got me sober in the first place. Someone really carrying a message, the kind I need to hear: the kind of message that once saved my life.

The way we're going to have to tear across the country and back I'm starting to wonder how free I am on this trip after all. These days it seems like you can have more freedom than ever before, as long as you have an abundance of two things: time and money.

While Jimmy obsessed about the first place we would stay in the US, he hasn't planned a thing beyond New Jersey and New York as far as I know. It's our own sort of recklessness, I suppose, just going with the flow, following the route of that first trip in *On the Road* and hoping the strangers we meet through AA will take care of us. Jimmy's one true focus now is to photograph the shit out of the places we visit. He's sure the next great photograph is there waiting for him.

We still haven't worked out how to cross the country yet. Neither of us wants to learn how to drive on the other side of the road in New Jersey or New York. I'm keen to wing it, but it's not all about me. I'm not Sal, I don't think everything will be better when we get to Denver just because it isn't where we are right now. I've got to consider where this bloke I'm travelling with might want to end up too. Right now that's Greenwich Village, so it's time to train it back to Manhattan.

When we get out of the subway, Jimmy remembers that the studio of a particular New York portrait photographer is nearby and steers us toward it. He tees up a quick meeting and we charge block to block into a more built-up part of Manhattan to make it. Jimmy finds the place in an area that is so damn New York it's ridiculous. We head past a doorman, whose wide-lapelled grey suit seems like the first uniform they gave him in the 80s, and head to the mission-brown lift. The photographer's assistant lets us in and I listen to Jimmy and the main guy here, Peter, talk shop for a minute. He's busy but is making some time for us between shooting an ape-like actor's semi-naked portfolio. While Peter photographs, his assistant, Pedro, comes and sits with us. He begins a strange monologue of hero worship, dismissing out of hand anyone who isn't at least Peter's assistant. He has no idea Jimmy's own photography business rakes it in and we can't be bothered educating him either, so we just let him go on and on. And on. Pedro is the first serious American wanker we've come across and I'm too excited to interrupt his wonderfully patronising flow. This makes the unexpected trip to the studio worth it. I can leave at any time but I want to stay and hear it all. I feel so free.

Jimmy is using a film camera he bought especially for the trip; like in the old days, you can't see the shot until you develop the film. With digital cameras we can see, delete, see, delete endlessly. But once you start doing that, the moment isn't fleeting any more, it becomes rehearsed, inauthentic. To live freely, you have to be in the moment. So while the digital camera has almost limitless capacity, there's less freedom and more restriction. Instant gratification, that's what digital gives. In my experience, there is no freedom in instant gratification. For an alcoholic or an addict, that's just putting your wrists out to be shackled. I'm a comfort junkie at heart; it's just that some comforts are far more damaging than others. I've never been kicked out of a café for drinking too much coffee.

•

After we leave the studio we head to a meeting Jimmy knows about in Greenwich Village. We walk down streets with names like Bleecker and 7th Avenue; even the street names here have permeated my memory from the sheer volume of American popular culture I absorbed growing up. Bob Dylan lived around here, Pollock too – the area is densely packed with the lives of musicians, painters and, more importantly for me, writers like Jack Kerouac. And smack in the middle is a building where there have been AA meetings for 50 years – meetings that so many of those artists just never made it into. Even if they did, there are no guarantees. An incredibly talented, successful actor living just down the street was a regular at this very meeting house before he scored his final hit and died. He's not the first and certainly won't be the last. Like I said, there are no guarantees in life, in or out of the AA rooms.

The opening line of the chapter 'Working with Others' in the AA Big Book states: 'Practical experience shows that nothing will so much insure immunity from drinking as intensive work with other alcoholics. It works when other activities fail.' *It works when all the other things fail*: like back-to-back episodes of the latest series, brutal exercise regimes and reading about mindfulness and being in the now. All great stuff, but they won't keep you sober the way talking to another alcoholic about alcoholism will. I'm keen to go to a meeting here for the simple reason that, no matter where I go in the world, I'm taking myself with me. And my mind has proven itself very skilled at skewing my perception of what is going on around me at any given time. I treat the disease of alcoholism like the disease of diabetes, and I didn't leave all my boxes of insulin in the fridge at home just because I was travelling.

The meeting starts at 12.15pm, so there's time to find a café I've read about that might solve my first-world, sober-man problem of 'needing' good coffee. That could be my biggest problem today. Not a hangover. Not a drunken car crash. Not a bank foreclosure or a black eye and missing teeth, or having to lie to my wife again about cheating on her again when I was drunk again. My biggest problem of the day could be finding someone here who can make a good flat white.

Bluestone Lane is right on Greenwich Avenue. The slim, dark-skinned girl takes my order from behind the counter. She's from Prahran in Melbourne and loving where she's working. Jimmy and I get talking to the waiter outside, a 20-something blond kid from Perth. He's on a student visa and the way he uses the word 'fun' when he describes working and living here alludes to a lot more than visiting the museums. It's too late for me, but I make a mental note to check in with my nephew back in Australia to try to convince him to relocate here for a spell while he's young and indestructible. I could barely get out of my street at his age. I had no idea how people did simple things like save for a trip. I've since learned that they didn't spend all their income on booze, cigarettes, taxis and fines.

Meetings have been happening in New York as long as anywhere else outside of Akron, Ohio. Still, the same things greet Jimmy and I as we arrive: smokers out the front, steps and traditions banners hanging on the walls inside. A framed sign reads: 'There is no wrong way to get sober.' The woman to my right leans in and asks me if I could cross my legs the other way as my leg is encroaching upon 'her space'. I'm definitely in the right place. She's been sober for only a few months and reminds me of me at that time, when you're so hypersensitive to the world that every tiny petty thing seems to have an impact, especially on your emotions.

I wonder how many addict artists have walked into this meeting house in Greenwich Village, decided it wasn't for them and died not long after. Addicted artists don't succeed because of their addiction but in spite of it. For every successful creative artist I can take you to a local pub and show you a drunken, drug-fuelled unmanageable mess who can't get any creative work done because they're always wasted. Then I'll take you to meet a creative professional who barely drinks, let alone takes anything else. I know from experience: I've been the sober one getting my shit done as well as the one at the pub achieving nothing.

Successful artists addicted to alcohol and drugs succeed for the same reasons tee-totalling creative artists succeed: brutal hard work and dedication to their craft, hour after hour, day after day, year after year. The truth is that Kerouac had the incredible work ethic of a prolific writer. The sadder truth is that he used alcohol and drugs to fuel it. The myth is that these alone are the muse that will bring you the great novel or the great album or the great performance, if only you'd quit the world and start taking them.

Booze and drugs have taken out a lot of famous names in my time and a long time before that: Amy Winehouse, whose biggest hit was about knocking back the help she so sorely needed, much as I like the way she said it; Oliver Reed, who died of an alcoholism-related heart attack; River Phoenix an overdose. Even Corey Haim was claimed by addiction. The booze got the better of Veronica Lake, Ryan Dunn of *Jackass* fame crashed his car drunk and John Bonham drank two bottles of vodka, went to bed and never woke up. But they're not the rule. Alice Cooper and Elton John gave it away and kept rocking, as did David Bowie and Eric Clapton. Rob Lowe is famously on the wagon, along with Alec Baldwin, Anthony Hopkins and Robert Downey Jnr.

At the Greenwich Village meeting, a young artist talked about working sober – just to do the work and be an artist. There must be hundreds like him, thousands. It wasn't until I regularly attended meetings that I got the picture: I wasn't special when it came to how I viewed the world. I'd heard of alcoholics having a 'big ego and low self-esteem' or feeling 'I'm the only person I think about, but I think I'm a piece of shit'. Sal Paradise reminds me of this state of mind. It's as if even the mundane ordinary experiences are exceptional because they're his, and no one else ever experienced them like he did. Nowhere in the writing does Sal stop to check with strangers at jazz gigs or bus stops to see if they're having an exceptional experience too. When you hear other people openly talking about how addiction plagued their lives, you get that sense of connection, of fellowship. Connection was probably what Carlo Marx wanted from his Benzo confessions with Dean Moriarty (aside from Dean himself).

Reading about the uniting powers of jazz and the divisive powers of bebop, and that sense of fellowship in the jazz clubs that brings them together, I remember having that too in those kinds of places – until the next day. When the night's over and you're hungover and alone again, you feel worse than before. Maybe you also feel a bit of guilt, or shame, or remorse, depending on what happened after the gig and who it happened with. This is the story that Sal is trying to tell, the misery that his friends feel individually and the shared ecstasy when they're playing up together and ignoring their differences. Though on the booze, that's easy – everyone is your friend when the beer is flowing and you can forget your normal life. Drugs more so – ecstasy especially. To be happy in this sense, Sal's sense, you must subordinate yourself to something bigger and do what they're all doing. But you could say that about a Klan rally and the people who get a sense of connection from attending those.

Still, the rooms of AA work the same way: people who are alone and miserable, and who feel they must be somehow different from those who can seemingly just handle life without drinking to excess, enter a room full of people who would not ordinarily mix. The stories that members share resonate; they share stories about wanting to feel connected to something, and how drinking gave them that feeling when they first started. We're all looking for a solution to the problem of disconnectedness. That's what the fellowship of

Alcoholics Anonymous is there for: to show you that you're not alone. When you identify so much with what another person is saying and what happened to them, it resonates so strongly that you feel like a part of something bigger. As Sal says, 'The atmosphere and I became the same.'

After the meeting I'm punching away at the subway ticket machine and I can hear a guy behind me rapping some old Biggie. He's got massive headphones on and he's loud and way off-key. He doesn't seem to mind. I turn around, sing the next line, 'now we sip champagne when we're thirstay', and he smiles and raps louder than before. I sing along as we go our separate ways. I'd bank on Kerouac digging the early 90s rappers in the way he dug the jazz players. No one used prose poetry and storytelling like those rappers did. As unschooled, underprivileged urban kids from parts of New York that had been all but abandoned, they used rhetorical devices better than White House speechwriters, bending the language to get their message heard.

Although Times Square is a recurring destination in *On The Road*, as are several other locales and streets in Manhattan, Queens, the Bronx and Brooklyn, I won't get to all of them on this trip, so I try to visit the prominent streets and see how things have changed since Kerouac wrote about them in the

50s. For now, going with the flow feels like the right thing to do; I don't have to control the flow. Jimmy is stopping at every store that he thinks might sell white T-shirts, telling me they're a particular passion of his. I think back and can't conjure a memory of him wearing anything else. He assures me it's not an obsession though, like his penchant for sitting in Starbucks.

I'm not at Hector's diner or the Chelsea Hotel, but we do get to the villages, where the city seems to calm down. We keep finding little inner-city car parks. This crowded city has schools behind fences between enormous buildings and even tiny cemeteries, but these car parks really stand out. Dean Moriarty was working in one in New York before they set out on the first trip, dodging and weaving in and out of the cars while he was shuffling them around the lot.

Early on in recovery, I worked as a labourer on the construction of the new long-term car park at Melbourne Airport. The workers were cliquey but I got paired up with an agency labourer who had a sense of humour and told good stories. He drove a shitbox Honda hatch with a cracked windscreen and kept a small baseball bat on the floor between the driver's seat and the door. I asked him what it was for and he replied, 'Oh, you need it where I live.' We worked as a pair and one day I watched people collecting their cars from the car park and paying to leave through the gate. I asked how much it cost. Turned out it was extortion compared to the bargain $50 cash I would charge to open up the handy construction gate for them instead. I told my buddy about my little scheme and his entrepreneurial drive was stronger than my conservative business plan of letting two cars out a week – he wanted 10 *per day*. He was thinking in profits of thousands of dollars. It was too much. We'd get caught.

And get caught we did, but not in the act. I got a call at home from the toad of a foreman, a man I couldn't stand. He asked me if I knew anything about anyone letting people out of the construction gate. As much as I wanted to tell this bloke to go fuck himself, I simply said, 'Yeah, I did it,' down the phone. It was like the part of me that knew how to lie had lost power or the part that told the truth had gotten stronger. I'd heard the words 'it's an honest program' so many times in AA meetings that I chose right there and then to be honest and that choice mattered. The foreman was livid. He yelled down the phone, 'Is anyone else doing it?' I said I couldn't speak for anyone else. Funny thing was, nothing bad happened from telling the truth. I didn't get paid that last week's pay, which was worth more than my enterprise had made in total, and understandably I was never asked back to work there. I have no idea if the other guy was questioned or what he said. It became history. Hope he doesn't need the baseball bat wherever he is now.

•

Given the way we'll be moving across country, and the timeframe we have to do it, writing 1000 words per day like I'd hoped just isn't going to happen. And I realise that unless I occasionally act independently of Jimmy, I'll soon get resentful as hell at stopping every two steps for photos or to spend hours in stores buying white T-shirts. I can do that at home, and I don't, so why would I do it here? Here, I've got a route to follow, put down 50 years ago.

For his first journey on the road, Sal rides the 7th Avenue subway up to the end of the line at 242nd Street in the Bronx, then hugs the Hudson River further north to Bear Mountain. I know Sal's false start is metaphorical and is the universe's way of correcting his course when, after intending west, he sheepishly travels north to nowhere, but still, he's looking for the answer 'out there'. Kerouac called *On the Road* 'a story about two Catholic buddies roaming the country in search of

God,' and wrote of himself, 'Am actually not "beat" but strange solitary crazy Catholic mystic.'

From my experience, when you're an alcoholic brought up Catholic, until you learn how to let go of the past, the only structure for God, for a higher power, for a universal creative force, is the religious one you have thrust upon you during your formative years: an angry old man in the clouds, strangely Anglo-Saxon-looking or even Nordic, as his son is often portrayed in Christian art. But the yearning for a connection with something else, whatever that may be, leads to all sorts of religious and spiritual misadventures, where you feel crazy and sound it too. It's Billy Bragg's 'sound of ideologies clashing', but internally. For Sal, the road becomes part of the higher power. Dean becomes part of the higher power. The girls and the jazz and the booze mesh into his higher power. It's a hell of a lot easier to hate a version of God handed to you than to formulate your own concept of a higher power and let that do what the original God was supposed to be doing, like looking out for you rather than judging your every failing and booking your ticket to hell.

I've heard it said that religious people don't want to go to hell, and spiritual people have been there and don't want to go back. Sal is looking for a connection with a power greater than himself and from time to time finds one, but only the human kind, which ultimately fails him. He's looking for freedom through faith, but he's putting his faith only in what will help him escape from freedom.

I don't say this out loud to Jimmy, I just ask him how he feels about driving and if we should do it yet. We discuss it and decide instead to get the train from New York to Pittsburgh and use this first trip to gauge how much time we'll take to get from place to place. Pittsburgh isn't a huge destination in *On the Road* and it's the same for us: an overnight stop on the way to Akron. Kerouac never passed through Akron but he skirted it when he went through Cleveland. I think of Sal's bus stopping in Akron and, on asking a passer-by for the nearest bar, him being directed to an AA meeting. So he goes. Imagine. That could have been disastrous for his drinking. No more road trips. No need to hit the road or look for 'it' out there. Jesus, imagine he took a service commitment and became the fucking secretary or something and never left. There would be no *On the Road* and I wouldn't be here following him. I never would have read his book, identified, and come all this way to follow his route west. I'd never have to challenge his notions of freedom. Or he might have looked around and walked straight back out again. Maybe he did just that and nobody knows.

Outside the station, Jimmy decides to take a couple of photos before we leave New York. He's clicking away and we hear, 'Hey, you need some colour in those pictures.' Reggie, from Brooklyn, talks like a street hustler out of a movie, and he didn't expect Jimmy to ask him if he could take his portrait. He's got his arms out, full swagger, for the camera, but after a few shots and a few words exchanged, his guard drops and Jimmy takes what he is sure will be the best portrait he has ever taken. Reggie drops the hustle and starts talking about why he's here at all on the streets of New York City. He's having trouble looking for work on account of a police record for being drunk. 'I just got some issues with drinking, you know, like everybody.' Everybody indeed. Seems like my world is revolving around issues with alcohol, be it ex-drunks or those who died from their drinking issues. Is anybody free from this shit?

Chapter Three

The carriage gently rocks out of Penn Station and despite the freezing temperature Amtrak has set the air conditioning to, we're both asleep in minutes. We wake just outside of Philadelphia. There's a stop here as a few disembark before the train changes direction westward, the conductor doubling as a tour guide while we're stationary.

'This is where the Founding Fathers signed the Declaration of Independence and the Constitution. It served as the capital before they built Washington, D.C., and it's also the spiritual home of cream cheese,' he says with a grin. I'd like to stay here a while and see the Liberty Bell and Georgetown and walk where Washington might have once walked while he contemplated the notion of a free country, but it isn't a stop that Sal or I factored into our journeys. Funny how we're off looking for freedom on the road without stopping in the city where the free country was founded. The old Amtrak diesel kicks into life again and the city of brotherly love peters out, giving way to lush Pennsylvania woodland.

In Pittsburgh, we meet a kid selling T-shirts featuring Mount Rushmore made up of Native American chiefs' faces, that read 'The *Original* Founding Fathers'. I ask him if anyone bothers him about selling them and he shakes his head. 'It's a free country,' he tells me in a scene too loaded for me to unpack. The next morning, we take the bus to Akron.

'Who is this guy who's meeting us?' Jimmy asks.

'His name is Edgar, Tim Ulrich got onto him for us.'

'Have you met him before?'

'No.'

'Have you ever met Tim before?'

'No.'

'How do you know he will show?'

'He'll be there. Haven't you ever given some random out-of-towner a lift after someone else asked you to?'

'Nup.' Jimmy laughs. 'We're getting into David Lynch territory out here.'

At Akron station, Jimmy piles the bags together and stands

guard over his camera. A white-haired man in a brown sedan waves over the steering wheel as he pulls up to the kerb. He steps straight out into the pelting rain, beaming, hand offered in welcome.

We get into the car and it's freezing like the train was. Edgar wastes no time in launching into a narrated tour as we head to the accommodation.

'Man oh man. I'm sure glad we're in here. This was tough to walk through back in the old days.'

'Walk through?'

'Oh yeah,' says Edgar, animated, 'I was a hobo.'

'What, like a homeless man?' asks Jimmy.

'I was a bona fide, box-car riding, hitchhiking, under-the-bridge hobo.'

Edgar says he crossed the country several times back and forth, not going anywhere special, just going. He reminds me of Sal's Ghost of the Susquehanna, the wet hitchhiker in old age. Edgar ended his hobo days by getting off the road some 20 years ago; he swapped the box-cars and bridges for the meeting rooms of AA. After a brief sight-see around Akron, Edgar drops us off at the motel and says to give him a call if we need anything. Nothing about him alludes to his former life of drunken destitution.

The risk of becoming homeless was a huge motivator for me to stop drinking. Realising that I'd made myself unemployable and had racked up a huge debt I could see no way of repaying scared the shit out of me. Pride and fear of what other people will think stops you from telling anyone how bad things have actually got. The build-up is gradual and suddenly, you're there – a step away from the guys holding brown paper bags with fingerless gloves in the park. I was sure I'd drop the insulin syringe and run out of reasons not to pick up one full of smack and if that happened, it's goodnight, Irene. That was about when I went to my first meeting.

•

Jimmy's sixth sense tells him there's a Starbucks across the road, but the lure of a Wal-Mart full of white T-shirts is stronger still. Under the motel awning we nearly bump into a rake-thin, wispy-haired man rolling a cigarette. I look him up and down for a moment and tell Jimmy to get his camera out, asking the man if we could take his portrait. He nods and, barely audible, gives his name as Robert. He leans toward the camera like he's pushing into a raging headwind; his skinny arms bend back behind his body, forearms straight down and ending in fists.

His furrowed brow lies somewhere between determination and confusion. After Jimmy is done, Robert quietly thanks us and rolls himself another cigarette. He is the ghost Sal talked about; a wind could blow through here and take Robert with it and no one would know. There'd only be Jimmy's portrait and an ashtray full of butts at the Akron Comfort Inn.

'That guy looks like what Edgar might if he was still a hobo,' says Jimmy.

'I think that's what either of us might look like soon if we start drinking again,' I say.

Jimmy scores himself a pack of Wal-Mart whities and we're soon inside a quiet Starbucks. Jimmy heads for a seat to look up some local car hire. Tian, the girl behind the counter, is chatty and I ask if she's travelled much through the US. She tells me she left Akron and went to live in New York for a few months but came back and has stayed ever since.

'You don't know there's no place like home until you leave it,' she says. If Dean is the perfect guy for the road, being born on the road, like Sal wrote, he must feel the way Tian just described when he's out of the car and living in an apartment.

I take a seat in the booth opposite Jimmy, who's staring out of the window at a car yard full of pickups.

'Any luck with the car hire?'

'Nup.'

'Does it matter? It's pretty shit weather to learn how to drive on the other side of the road.'

'Yeah but still, it would be good to get a car and just drive.'

'You wanna pick up a hire car then?'

'I'm thinking about it. Let's keep an eye out for a hire place.'

We get up from our booth and head out to cross the road. Maybe it's the thought of a car, or the car yard opposite has mesmerised him, but Jimmy plants a foot on the road before turning his head, pulling himself back a second before a car hurtles past blasting its horn.

'Fuck. I just didn't look,' he says. 'I forgot they come from the other direction over here. Fuck.'

'You all right?'

'Let's just get the bus into town.'

I've let him know that Sal got the bus all the way to Denver and beyond and then got the bus back again all the way from San Francisco to New York, but that knowledge is little comfort. I'm not Sal Paradise and Jimmy's not Dean Moriarty, but we could at least get our shit a bit more together when it comes to getting on the road in a car. In defeat, we meekly head across the road to the bus stop.

We're talking to each other about the bus route and the young guy sitting in the shelter asks, 'Are you guys from Australia?'

'Yeah.'

'That's fucking awesome! I've never met an Australian!'

His name is Ryan, and he's a local guy, Akron born and bred. He asks us what we're doing here and I tell him about following the route from *On the Road* and writing about freedom. He tells us that today is his first day of freedom in a long time. He's been in prison for a couple of years and it's literally his first day out, he's on his way home. I let slip that my version of freedom is about doing the trip sober.

'Sober?' he asks. 'Like, AA sober?'

'Yeah,' I say.

Ryan sits back and looks from me to Jimmy and back a couple of times. 'You guys are really AA members from Australia?'

'Yeah,' I tell him, 'that's why we stopped in Akron.'

Ryan nods and tells us he went to jail for drug and alcohol offences and started going to meetings while he was in there. He's been sober for eight months now even though he could get whatever he wanted in prison. The bus arrives and we all get on, still talking.

'Don't stop living,' Ryan says. He's lost his freedom before, in a couple of ways, and doesn't want to lose it again. I ask him what his plans are and what he wants to do. He says he wants to become a warehouse manager now he has his high school certificate, but deep down he wants to be a screenwriter. I like this kid. He sounds like me, just younger; I got sober and started working in construction and warehouses but deep down wanted to try my hand at writing.

'Another year of probation is not that big a deal compared to being in prison,' he says. 'I prayed this morning to be shown if I'm doing the right thing. Then two sober Australians show up at the bus stop to escort me into town, talking about freedom! Something is listening to those prayers, man. Something. For sure.'

I feel like Sal on the back of the track to Denver, meeting the like-minded guys on the way to the harvest. We don't share a bottle of whiskey with Ryan but we connect through our stories.

'So are you guys here for the 80th anniversary?'

'The what?'

'AA's 80th anniversary week. Today is Founders' Day.'

The AA guys who came to Ryan's prison told him about the 80th anniversary events dotted around town, and how he might meet out-of-towners this week, but he's stoked to meet Australians. Jimmy and I look at each other and laugh nervously. We had no idea.

Anniversaries mean different things to different people, and AA is no different. To some, this day is momentous; to others, it's just another day in their own sobriety. Regardless, it was in Akron, 80 years ago, that a former chronic alcoholic named Bill Wilson realised that he could stay away from a drink if he could find another alcoholic to talk to. In desperation, Bill made a series of phone calls and found Dr Bob Smith, a local physician with a similar problem. According to the annals of AA literature and folklore, they talked and talked and Bill shared his experience and Bob stopped drinking. Bill Wilson managed to stay sober for six months by talking at unresponsive drunks on skid row, but didn't find a reciprocating person until he met Bob. They both stayed sober, then worked together to successfully help others get sober in a fashion similar to the modern AA structure. That's why the first word in each of the Twelve Steps is 'We'. The day of Dr Bob's sobriety was pinned as the beginning of Alcoholics Anonymous.

They weren't the first to happen upon a way to get sober that included meeting regularly with other alcoholics. There had been the Temperance movement and the Washingtonians and the Oxford groups, but what these two guys and the first 80-odd other people who were involved at the start did differently was to make it just about alcoholism and nothing else – and write it all down. They didn't even have a name for their fellowship until after they came up with the title Alcoholics Anonymous for the basic text itself. After a while the nickname 'Big Book' caught on and it's been called that ever since.

Ryan heads home and we head to the University of Akron where they have setup for Founder's Day week. It's a gathering point for the local AA groups to have bigger meeting rooms and spread a selection of anniversary literature on tables and generally mill around talking to one another. There are plenty of memorial tokens, like 80-year AA chips, copies of books you don't usually see at regular meetings, old-school Golden Books with titles like *The Golden Book of Sponsorship* by Father John Doe, stamped on the inside cover with the 80-year Founders' Day stamp.

I have no idea who Father John Doe is or if he was even an AA member, but I remember my sponsor Ken talking about these Golden Books and how they were widely read by AA members in the US. Jimmy picks up a copy of *The Best of Bill*, selected anecdotal writing by Bill Wilson and tells me this'll do him.

'You want to go to a meeting here?' I ask.

'Nah, not really, I've had enough for one day,' he says. 'I'll take some photographs in town.'

I assumed Jimmy would be keen to catch a meeting in the town where it all started but he doesn't seem at all interested. I thought it was a given but he's right; it's not a religion, there are no rules. We're not in Bethlehem or Mecca, though the way I've thought about coming here, we may as well be. Maybe Jimmy has more of handle on being free here than I do.

•

When I was first getting sober, it was straightforward to accept Step One (that I was powerless over alcohol), and Step Two (that maybe something bigger could restore me to sanity). My sponsor told me to pray every morning, to whatever might be out there, that I could be of service to others and that I might have the willingness to do whatever it takes to stay sober. He said it didn't matter who or what I thought God was, as long as I knew it wasn't me. That was a relief, I can tell you. It was a step in the direction of being restored to sanity; just to get out of my own head in a non-destructive way. I needed a god but had long since given up on the Catholic God of my upbringing. I heard a few other ideas in meetings, like the acronyms Good Orderly Direction or Group Of Drunks, but I knew I needed something with a bit more clout than a meeting of well-meaning guys who were off the sauce.

At the beginning of the second trip in *On the Road*, Dean says 'And of course now no one can tell us that there is no God,' followed by 'Everything is fine, God exists, we know time ... And not only that but we both understand that I couldn't have time to explain why I know and you know God exists.' Did Dean mean the Catholic God or was he talking about his own idea of what it could be? I was being given an opportunity to make a decision on what it could be, but AA's third step isn't so much about what it is or even its existence. Step Three reads: 'Made a decision to turn our will and our lives over to the care of God *as we understood Him*.'

Knowing sounds great, but Step Three is placing the responsibility in my hands to decide to place the outcome of my actions in the hands of something else, something bigger than me and my limitations. It's frightening, yet liberating. Instead of rebelling against someone else's ideas, I could take responsibility and come up with my own. The less human, the better. No old man in the sky with the worst of human traits; far removed from the Greek or Roman gods who carry on like brats from a reality TV show. I settled on the idea of a universal creative force that I can't possibly fathom and that I don't *have* to fathom; I just ask it to handle the outcome after I put in the actions. The implication is that I can't sit on my hands and expect things to be handed to me. I have to constantly take action, use my will and live my life, but let go of the idea that controlling the result is within my power.

Really, who cares what this higher power actually is anyway? It's what it does that's important. Like my friend Tommy used to say, 'God can move mountains, if you're willing to show up with a shovel and start digging.' It sounds insane that, in this day and age of modern medicine and science, that was the suggestion and I went with it. Maybe one day science will explain how I stopped drinking and then I'll have different words to explain what God as we understood Him is, like gravity or magnetism or some other eternal, permeating force that acts in the background of all our lives.

My sponsor also said to keep calling him regularly and to keep calling other alcoholics. Lots of them. 'You've got to get honest,' he'd say, 'and one of the easiest ways to practise being honest is to be forthcoming with the truth on a regular basis.'

He also said, 'It's great to have friends in AA. Just remember, they could be drunk tomorrow – and so could I. So get to know lots of people and get a prospective sponsor on the bench.'

They were telling me at meetings to 'just keep coming back' and, before I got the sack for pulling the car park scam, they were saying the same thing at the construction site. They kept paying me to stand around taking a laser level every half an hour. They didn't care what happened between my ears, they were interested in what I did in front of their eyes. But the work dried up and I fell into a familiar pattern of taking cash advances out on my credit cards to pay for things. That's how I'd lived in my last few months of drinking: get up in the afternoon, take out cash from an ATM, use the money to buy booze, maybe drugs, get smashed, repeat. Now the getting-smashed part had stopped, but the behaviour with the money lingered, because I thought using money I didn't have – to pay for 'good' things – made it okay.

I joined a boxing gym in the hope to burn up excess energy and the endorphin hit had me hooked pretty quickly; it didn't take long before I was training for at least an hour, nearly every afternoon. In the early sobriety state of mind that isn't quite sanity, it seemed inevitable that the next logical step was a boxing career.

One day on the way to the gym, it occurred to me that I didn't have the 20 bucks I needed to pay for training that week. Not one dollar spare of cash. I had committed to AA principles about being willing to change and take different actions, and I had sworn off my old MO of taking a cash advance on the credit card. Something I'd never heard before AA was that alcoholics have to take the action first to make their thinking change, not the other way around. It explains a lot of my past behaviour and broken promises. It was like that first night I drove past the bottle shop when I could hear Shane's voice saying, 'Sometimes it's a minute at a time,' or when I was on the phone to the foreman about the airport car park and told the truth instead of lying. It's in those kind of moments where real change happens.

As I made my way to the gym I started to justify my plan: I'm not in the temple; I'm not on the mountaintop; I'm not high in San Francisco. But I am on the road. I'm in my car, in a familiar situation; I'm going to a place I've been before, about to do something that, although seemingly small in the grand scheme of things, I know is not a good thing to do for myself. I justify it further: I'm not drinking or smoking, I'm taking care of my health, I'm training at the gym. What's the big deal? It's only 20 bucks. I'll do something about it tomorrow. Except I'm going to AA because I thought I was going to die if I didn't stop drinking and they repeat like a broken record 'one day at a time is how you do it'. Don't drink just for today. Just go to a meeting today. Do the thing today. And I'm all for it, I've been saying it out loud in meetings for weeks. They also keep saying it's an 'honest' program. There are three kinds of dishonesty for people like us, they tell me: lying, not being forthcoming with the truth or lying by omission, and living in delusion. And they told me to ask for help, especially from a power greater than me. So I did. I prayed from behind the wheel of a car at a red light, looking up at the sky through the windscreen.

'Now look, do you want me to do this or not? Is this okay or not? Is this your will for me or not? It seems to be, so, look, this is what I'm going to do: I'm going to drive to the gym and I'm going to pull into the petrol station near the gym. Then, I'm going to get out and go in and get 20 bucks from one of the credit cards. Then I'm going to the gym and I'm paying for this week's training. Then I'll pay it back and try not to do this any more and pay back my debt when I can. And if that's your will for me, or if it's not, fucking show me.'

I drove another couple of minutes and pulled into the petrol station. No other cars. Quiet for this time of the day. Inside, no other customers. The place was empty.

I step up to the teller machine and take out the credit card and nearly insert it. Then I notice a 20 on the tray where the notes are dispensed. A crisp, solitary, $20 bill. The exact amount I was about to withdraw. I picked it up and held it in front of me for a second with the credit card in the other hand, looking from one to the other. I went over to the counter saying, ‘Hello, hello?’ in case the clerk was doing stuff and I couldn’t see him, but no one was there. Where the fuck was the guy who worked here? No one was outside. No one had left as I came in. The money was just there, waiting for me. No one came in, not even the clerk.

I’d asked for this. Not five minutes before, I’d asked to be shown. I didn’t pray for the money, I prayed for knowledge of that higher power’s will for me, specifically. Consider myself shown. Or it was just an incredibly coincidental, extremely unlikely, massively odd occurrence. I’ve used ATMs hundreds of times all around the world and nothing like that has happened before or since. I went to the gym, telling no one, saying nothing.

I sat in meetings for weeks thinking about what had happened and itching to share it, but I didn’t get asked to. But I didn’t even tell anyone when I had the chance. The fact that it happened to me just like that wasn’t enough to crack my cynical idea that if someone tells you a story like that, they're just trying to sell you something. I think I dropped the story of the $20 bill for the first time at a spiritual concept meeting when I got sick of hearing about yoga and Eckhart Tolle.

•

Back at the motel in Akron, Jimmy and I burn up some of that excess alcoholic energy that just seems to accumulate when you're sober with a bit of exercise and get a nice endorphin buzz. When you don't drink, smoke or do anything else, you take what you can get. We ask the receptionist at the check-in counter where to go for a good meal and she points us to a sports bar down the road past the vast expanse of the Wal-Mart car park. Jimmy is upbeat after lifting a few weights and even mentions it might be worth calling Edgar and seeing a few of the historical AA sites tomorrow if he's around and willing to drive us. The gym and the walking around has worked up our appetites and we get a nice corner table outside in the Akron warmth, putting away the biggest and best Reubens we've ever seen as the other patrons drink beer and watch football on big outdoor screens.

The next morning, Edgar pulls up outside the motel right on time and drives us to Dr Bob's house at 855 Ardmore Avenue. It's a museum of sorts now, but it's still pretty much a regular house in a regular street in a regular American suburb. Edgar launches into a lament about the people we can see selling T-shirts and some other kind of merchandise nearby, but drops it completely as soon as we're walking toward the house. He counts the stairs as we walk up to the front door: '... 10, 11, 12.' I can't tell if there are really twelve steps or if Edgar is taking the piss, but he's beaming as he holds the door open for us.

Inside, the house is full of visitors. It is, after all, the 80-year anniversary of AA and there are a hell of a lot of people in AA who live within a short drive of Akron. There's a coffee pot on the kitchen table, the fabled coffee pot that Bill Wilson and Dr Bob and others whose names I've never bothered to look up used to gather around. I wonder how long it took Lois Wilson to gather all their wives together and form Al-Anon, the worldwide group that helps those affected by alcoholism. There are strategically placed early editions of AA literature on side tables in the downstairs rooms and little notes about them. A Bible too, not surprisingly, seeing as Bill and Bob used the Christian Oxford groups as an initial template. Upstairs are a couple of drying-out rooms for detoxing alcoholics, with some medicinal relics from the era. This is nothing like the organised, structured meeting I first walked into, but this is where it all started and this is where the AA fellowship and the message it carries started to take shape.

'My writing is teaching,' Kerouac wrote in his journal. This was the point of *On the Road*, even if readers didn't get it at first. The Big Book has the same point, to teach the reader how to get sober the way it worked for the early AA members. Kerouac wrote: 'One of the greatest incentives of the writer is the long business of getting his teachings out and accepted.' If his writing is teaching, what is he teaching? The 25-year-old's guide to running away? The disposable nature of the post-World War Two woman?

It's easy to glean abstract lessons hidden in the chaos of disjointed and spontaneous road travel set at a cracking pace. The biggest lessons don't reveal any secrets to freedom, though. The lessons are that you can write some damn good prose in your mid-twenties and you can resonate with readers of a certain age at a certain time. I might have read *On the Road* as a sober man in my mid-thirties and seen nothing but the kind of behaviour that lands people in AA. But when I was in my early to mid-twenties, when I was engaging in similar destructive behaviour, I might have identified with Sal and Dean in a totally different way and be defending the book against an older, sober, boring, self-righteous version of myself who was sucking all the fun out of an American classic. What a fucking square!

The message Bill Wilson wrote in *Alcoholics Anonymous*, published in 1939, was pretty direct. But it wasn't written as literature. It was written as a textbook on how to practically go about arranging a personal spiritual experience, which, according to those who got sober in early AA, is necessary to remove the desire for drinking alcohol. Kerouac's writing, not as blatant about its purpose, seemed to point in the same direction – using travels on the road to arrange a personal spiritual experience, but without the idea that alcoholism was the problem at hand. Kerouac's problems at hand were the restlessness and discontentedness that came with alcoholism, the symptoms manifested in his surrounding circumstance. His message is about searching for a spiritual solution, but a solution to what exactly remains a mystery behind his beautiful prose.

On the Road and the Big Book survive because they give readers something they can use, something they can identify with. In Bill's own story, the desire to run away from the passage of growing up – or the desire to obliterate it altogether – is quite clear. It's the same for Sal's journey. The difference is the Big Book gives you a way out, written in practical language with little myths and metaphors. Literally written in steps.

•

Edgar shows us to Dr Bob's gravesite and offers to take our photo by the headstone, which Jimmy and I agree is weird and a little creepy, but we do it anyway. I'm sure Jim Morrison fans do this in Paris every day but it's, yeah, odd. He drives us past the huge Seiberling mansion where Bill Wilson lived as a guest for a while and we drive into town to visit the Mayflower Hotel, the place where they say Bill made a few phone calls before he eventually made the one that got him in touch with Dr Bob. Jimmy gets some shots of the foyer, which looks like it hasn't been touched since Bill was here.

The last stop on Edgar's homemade tour is the St Thomas Hospital Chapel, now laid out with glass cabinets housing photographs and information. Edgar recounts the story of the good Samaritan, depicted in one of the leadlight windows, comparing the alcoholic with all his past faults changing them into assets he can help others with. His eyes well up and he stutters a few words. Jimmy is a deer in headlights. As I pat Edgar's shoulder and wonder what to do next, he suddenly animates with the words, 'From hopeless drunks to saviours of the hopeless,' and gives us that big, dimpled, close-lipped smile he had on when he collected us from the bus depot.

'All right, you fellas ready to go?' he says, clapping his hands together.

We nod and follow him out the door.

'Mate, I'm glad you put your hand on his shoulder then, I didn't know what to do,' says Jimmy.

'I think he's just right into it, you know? He was a bum once. A real one, a skid-row hobo with a drinking problem. Now he's got a nice house, a wife, he shows people around his town. I think he's just grateful.'

'He lives and breathes it,' says Jimmy. He's got a thousand-yard stare as we follow Edgar out of the hospital.

Back in the car, Edgar takes a call and puts it on loudspeaker. The guy on the other end of the line says something about missing his regular meeting and Edgar says, 'I'll come over and put a foot in your ass.' He's laughing. 'You're on loudspeaker with a couple of Aussies in my car, by the way.'

We can't make out what the other guy is saying and Edgar throws in the odd 'shit' and 'fuck' and then winds it up with,

'All right. I love you, man,' before hanging up and shaking his head. 'Old sponsee,' he tells us. He drops us at the motel and shakes our hands firmly. 'If you boys are ever back in the area, just let me know you're coming.'

'Likewise, Edgar. If you ever make it on a plane to Australia, let me know and we can show you around.'

'You never know in this show,' he says. 'You just never know.'

Jimmy raises his eyebrows as we head into the motel and book ourselves seats on the next bus to the Motor City, via Cleveland.

Chapter Four

'Now I take it y'all ain't from around here,' says the bus driver, stopping us at the door in Cleveland. 'Australians?' His eyebrows seem to be doing the talking over the top of bifocals perched on the end of his nose. His nametag reads 'Milton Leverette' and he is everything you could want in a Greyhound driver. If the role of playing Morgan Freeman is ever up for grabs, Milton is the man for the job.

Jimmy takes his photograph and Milton manages to pose without posing. At the same time, he gives me his take on freedom. 'Being able to live the way I want to live,' he tells me. Sounds pretty sweet, unless you're Ted Bundy or Jeffrey Dahmer, I suppose. Milton announces that the PA isn't working, which I suspect is a ruse to get everyone to listen up when he's delivering instructions. We take a seat opposite an Ice Cube lookalike who chews a toothpick and flicks a nod our way. Jimmy sticks in his headphones and pulls out a copy of Don Watson's *American Journeys*. Don't know how he does it – I was never any good at reading with headphones in.

While we've exercised a little tourist street-smarts kind of caution in Cleveland, there's been nothing to be afraid of. Everything dangerous I've seen in the local papers or on the news seems to happen late at night or around drugs and alcohol, situations we avoid by default of being sober. We're up early and asleep by 10 or 11pm, which may sound soft, but both of us have seen the inside of plenty of bars, clubs and dives and there's a hell of a lot more to see in this country than drinking establishments.

Kerouac described living – and writing about living – as being 'the work'. This is a job, so I'm at work right now, just without the weekly pay cheque and accumulating annual leave. On a bus between Cleveland and Detroit, rolling through the green fields of Ohio, passing through settings, engaging with characters, plot unfolding.

The bus rolls into the terminal in Toledo, and a few passengers get off, including the intimidating Cube-alike. He's immediately replaced by an awkward, gangly, side-burned kid, who bumps into everyone still seated as he makes his way down the aisle. He drops anchor opposite me and Jimmy and immediately tries to engage us.

'I'm going to Detroit. I'm willingly on a bus heading to Detroit,' he says, looking around and nodding in imaginary agreement with everybody at the foolishness of such an idea. On a bus full of people headed to Detroit. My first thought is: If we speak to this guy, we will be stabbed purely by association. I don't want either, the stabbing or the association. But it's like he sees us as kin, the only other 30-something white guys on this bus.

He enthusiastically tells us he's from Montreal and is headed to Detroit for a party, reminding us and the rest of the bus, again, that he is willingly heading there as if it is akin to heading to the dentist and enthusiastically refusing painkillers for a root canal.

I pump out thought-waves informing everyone on the bus we have nothing to do with this fuckwit. I'm also sorely disappointed with the first Canadian we've met on the trip. I'd always considered Canadians to be the New Zealanders of the United States, and expat New Zealanders are among the finest people on the planet. Now Montreal is forever tainted as the home of this guy, and possibly countless like him, and we are tainted on this bus because we talked to him. Jimmy severed ties in seconds, pushing his earphones in deeper and staring straight at the back of the seat in front of him, expressionless. I panicked, and continued to answer Mr Montreal in monotone.

Then I heard the voice of the Lord. And the Lord sayeth, 'Y'all in my seat.' Cube is back. I look at Cube, then Mr Montreal, then Jimmy, with a smile. Mr Montreal looks Cube up and down and promptly stands up, bumping into the overhead rack as he snatches at his bag, pulling it down onto himself and tumbling out into the aisle. Cube effortlessly slides into position opposite us, chewing his toothpick, flicking another nod. Jimmy removes an earpiece and coolly acknowledges this as evidence that we're being looked after by a higher power. We settle in for the rest of the journey from Toledo to Detroit, confident we're in the right place.

•

Our Panama-born cab driver, Dan, says, 'Freedom means I can be president!' as he drops us off at our bland, no-brand hotel. Manning the reception is Latoja, Detroit born and raised, who will come to refer to us as 'those nice Australians'.

'As a woman,' she says, 'freedom means stability, power, voting rights, equal opportunity and independence.' Tim, the waiter in the diner next door, is working the Sunday breakfast shift and has three daughters at home. 'If they're happy, I'm happy,' he assures me. 'You got to work for your happiness, but if you're happy, you're free.' This diner is everything we wanted and didn't get in Pittsburgh or Akron. A waitress in an apricot dress with a classic white apron pours coffee into an actual ceramic cup and there's real metal cutlery. We're in a low-backed booth that seems tailor-made to join in conversation with the next booth.

Michael and Tom are middle-aged former Greyhound drivers. They talk passionately about all topics from collectable buses to freedom. 'No restrictions, enjoying life,' is Michael's take on freedom, while Tom adds, 'No restrictions on travel.' They just may have got it too, in a job that paid them to hit the road every day. I'm enjoying being in the booth next to these guys – a big, round, white-haired white guy and a little, round, black-moustachioed black guy, sitting together, talking about freedom. I get a buzz out of how authentically American this feels.

Our neighbours in the hotel are four buddies from Lansing, in town for the baseball, who confess to having seen 'fuck all of the USA', but they love to drink beer and smoke weed. It reminds us that we saw fuck all of the world when we used to drink beer and smoke weed too. A guy called Mike does most of the talking and at one point passes the window holding a massive spliff between his fingers. 'Smoky, smoky?'

Another time I would've lit it before he stopped talking, got drunk with him and his buddies, and then likely gotten mugged in the wrong part of town while attempting to buy speed, ecstasy or cocaine. 'No, thanks,' I tell him.

Mike's spin on freedom is succinct. 'Don't be afraid. You can't live your life afraid. If you do, you're not living your life.' In my experience, he's right. In my drinking days, fear stopped me from doing anything with my life. Drinking alleviates a lot of that fear, but leaves you too drunk to do anything about it. There's still fear when you're sober – I just get to be aware of it and do something about it. Mike asks if we can send him a photo of the Pacific Ocean when we get there, so I take down his email address.

We hail a cab to take us to an AA meeting. We're not sure we're heading in the right direction, and the meter seems to be spinning out of control, so we tell the driver to pull over and let us out. He deliberately keeps going and drops us off further up the road, opposite a yard where four guys in do-rags sit drinking out of brown paper bags around a fire. I'm thinking, *Shit suddenly got serious.* Jimmy's face tells me the same tape is playing in his head too. That fucking cab driver. He knew this was a dodgy street. I'm never getting into a cab again. Maybe it serves us right for not manning up and getting a fucking car in the city that used to make most of them. Bloody cab drivers. They don't deserve my resentment.

The Big Book says, 'Resentment is the "number one" offender. It destroys more alcoholics than anything else. From resentment stems all forms of spiritual disease, for we have been not only mentally and physical ill, we have been spiritually ill. When the spiritual malady is overcome, we straighten out mentally and physically.'

For an alcoholic, resentment is a feeling of bitter indignation at the perception of having been treated unfairly, which is played in the mind, over and over and over again. You are entertained, fed, kept alive by thinking about the injustice; you have that 'I'm gonna say this, then they will say this, then I will ...' crazy kind of prediction of how the next meeting with the resented person will pan out. It doesn't go away of its own accord either. Ironically, it can be in the familiarity of the AA meetings that these petty resentments really fester if you don't keep a check on yourself.

This is what personal inventory is for. Step Four reads: 'Made a searching and fearless moral inventory of ourselves.' Firstly, it says ourselves, not anyone else, which alcoholics seem adept at. It's not the cab driver, it's me. I got angry with him; he didn't really do anything but be a cab driver. The other thing to note is that many, many alcoholics baulk at this step and start drinking again. I once sponsored a guy named Jeff who got this far and then decided he needed a new sponsor rather than go through with it. It's jokingly referred to as the 'AA waltz'. Steps one, two, three, one, two, three ... It's funny, except for the times when, like Jeff, rather than progress through the steps or go back to drinking, people kill themselves.

So you start writing down all your resentments. All of them. One by one. For some this is a long, long list. For Sal, it might start with his mother, then his father. An ex. Another ex. Someone from college. Someone from the military. This is the stuff that gets carried around and covered over, the stuff alcoholics drink on. Resentments and harms and fears, they all get written down.

I remember the first time I put all these resentments on paper. I didn't like what I saw, but it was a major step towards freedom – a bridge, if you like. I could start living free instead of talking about living free or only feeling free when I was drinking. But I realised that all that resentment and fear had really been running my life.

Kerouac once wrote that he was torn between a side of himself that he described as 'the introverted, scholarly side; the alien side, and 'the halfback-whoremaster-alemate-scullion-jitterbug-jazz critic side.' It reminds me of all the recovering alcoholics I've listened to in meetings describe their acquired sense of connection that comes from a few drinks. From a square peg in a round hole to the life of the party. Get a few beers into Jack and he's a different man. Maybe a better one? Surely more fun to be around. Then one day the drink stops working its magic and turns him into the annoying, loud, difficult, dysfunctional, drunk pain in the arse.

The two sides Kerouac talks about sounds to me like the fractured mental world of an alcoholic: never complete, putting up different masks to handle life with different people. Fear-driven, people-pleasing, worried what others think and having an ego that needs to prove something, full of pride out front but sensitivity and lack of self-esteem internally, with a double dose of emotions.

In the rooms of AA, one of the terms you'll hear from time to time is getting 'right sized' and 'I'm just a grain of sand on the beach – but if it wasn't for each grain of sand like me, there wouldn't be a beach.' No more polar extremes, but a contented middle ground. The ground where you can have fulfilling relationships with your fellow human beings.

After you write the resentments, you look resolutely for your own mistakes, not in *the* world, but your own world. When you have all your resentments and harms and fears in four columns, the last columns are the ones that answer this question: Where were we to blame? When alcoholics get to this point and refuse to go any further, it's known as 'baulking at Step Four'. It's the fear that comes from knowing that, in all those situations that didn't work out or when someone got hurt or something was lost or broken or destroyed, the one common denominator was your involvement. So in my life, to a part, it is my fault. It is my responsibility.

Would Kerouac have recoiled from Step Four? In *On the Road*, they call it the urinal scene: 'I don't know what to do with these things. I hold things in my hand like pieces of crap and don't know where to put it down.' Sal follows this later: 'It's not my fault!' he says. 'Nothing in this lousy world is my fault, don't you see that? I don't want it to be and it can't be and it won't be.'

For me, the urinal scene is Sal's ultimate tantrum, his refusal to grow into adulthood. Acceptance that you must live life on life's terms, not exclusively on your own terms, is paramount if an alcoholic ever hopes to get any freedom and joy out of life while sober. There's not much to say when a man in his mid-twenties throws all his toys out of the pram and shakes his little fists, crying. There is no real absolution or forgiveness in confession. Even if there were, it doesn't matter: absolution and forgiveness don't stop the same behaviour from happening again, they really only encourage it. The great touchstone of growth is pain, and if someone is constantly patted on the head and forgiven, the bottle shoved back in their mouth, they never will grow up. Their body might get bigger and capable of far more destruction, but the contents of the bottle will change from milk to booze.

Would Dean Moriarty have recoiled from Step Four? Kerouac's lifelong friend Ed White (known by the moniker Tim Gray in *On the Road*) had known Neal Cassady, the real Dean Moriarty, in Denver and thought he was full of it. Tom Livornese, a friend who opened his apartment to Cassady and his child bride, LuAnne, found Dean's constant talking 'an astronomic con of the worst sort'. But Kerouac seemingly wanted to be bullshitted. He needed it. In *On the Road*, Sal says, 'He was conning me and I knew it ... and he knew I knew (this has been the basis of our relationship).' Neither of them are totally honest with each other. They are as dependent on each other in the same way they are dependent on booze and drugs and sex to feel okay. Well, sane and sober people have no place on the road with these two – they see straight through them. They don't buy into the drama and the lies, but most of all, they see through the justification and the guise.

Ed White and Tom Livornese sound like the kind of people I would have thought were wankers when I was drinking. Then, when I got sober, they would have popped up in my fourth step and I would have had to acknowledge my mistake, my part, in any resentment toward them. The truth would probably have been that I was afraid of them holding up a mirror I didn't want to look at. My fear would have overridden their honesty and sober reasoning.

Me and Jimmy are holed up in a pizza place near where the cabbie dumped us waiting for a replacement cab to take us back to our accommodation. We forget all about going to the meeting. Derek, our new cabbie, is a nervous-looking kid with short curly brown hair and a light sweat. He's planning to move to Portland to get away from the 'negative attitude' in Detroit after the demise of the car manufacturing industry.

'You should be free to buy and smoke weed here like cigarettes,' he says. 'Everyone is smoking it anyway. It could replace cars as the new industry.'

Once we're out of the car, Jimmy declares Derek more negative than the demise of the auto industry. 'What an arsehole,' he says. 'What about the old drivers from the diner and the receptionist and cops? They're all positive. This guy is the negative vibe. Why don't you piss off to Portland then?' Jimmy made a connection with Detroit long before we got here, and now he's defending the place like he was born and bred here. I love it.

•

'What day is it?'

I'm in the back of an ambulance with Jimmy and a paramedic, en route to the hospital. By the time I'm admitted, I've pieced together what happened. We were wandering around Greek Town when I started to get that jelly-legged, dizzy feeling that means I'm running on low blood sugar. According to Jimmy, I started charging towards a 7-Eleven mumbling, 'Sugar, sugar,' but just conked out on the sidewalk. I interpret the fact that I passed out in downtown Detroit and emerged with my wallet intact – with each of my five-dollar bills undisturbed – a sign that I'm being taken care of by larger forces. And Jimmy was with me the whole time, of course. Watching me pass out can't have been fun for him to witness. Luckily I'd told him on the plane what to do if I have any diabetic trouble.

It had been a strange day – we seemed denied at every turn. It rained, so Jimmy didn't want to shoot. The bookstore I wanted to check out was closed. Even the Nike store with the ridiculous chalk Air Max we both wanted closed early.

When I'm discharged from the hospital, we head back to town determined to make sure the evening isn't a total wipeout. Downtown is throbbing with classic cars: Challengers, Camaros, Mustangs, all lit up like Christmas trees. Then there are motorbikes nearly as wide as the cars and with bigger sound systems. Jimmy is fired up now and keen for action.

In *On the Road*, Sal and Dean immerse themselves in poverty in an all-night theatre on Detroit's skid-row. We don't even find a skid-row, not that we look that hard for one. When Kerouac was in college, he chose to immerse himself in poverty-stricken Detroit just for the writing experience. It's a lot easier to identify with the gutter when you refuse to grow up and identify with the adults. Maybe that paragraph is the main reason Detroit was kept in the book.

In the unedited scroll draft, where Sal and Dean are still going by their real names of Jack and Neal, Kerouac fell asleep in the all-night theatre and had to have the evening reported back to him by Cassady. Me, I hit the pavement from a hypo and blacked out in downtown Detroit and the ambulance took me to the local hospital. Thank God I was sober and sane enough to have travel insurance.

After dinner and a look around, Detroit doesn't reveal itself like we hoped it might and we throw in the towel early for a Saturday night.

•

Checking out of the hotel, I'm annoyed that we're so close to the Canadian border but are not going to cross it. Jimmy is disappointed in Detroit. We go into town, me with my backpack and Jimmy with his tiny camera bag and 50 white T-shirts. In the Hudson Café on Brightmoore, we're served by a diminutive waitress named Madison who is all glasses and hoop earrings and quite happy to chat with us about Detroit. She and her partner bought a house here for around $5000. I can't help but ask her about the high level of crime and whether she feels safe.

'Every place is as safe as you are smart,' she replies. Fair enough, it's not like she's skulking about the hood at 3am buying crack. Freedom, Madison says, means 'I don't have to answer to anyone else. When I'm detached from authority and kinda making up my own.' Sounds good too, until her manager comes over and tells her to get back to work.

After a stack of pancakes and coffee, Madison lets us leave our shit at the café while we ride the monorail. It might be a sad reflection on us but we're pretty fucking psyched about catching the monorail, quietly chanting, 'Monorail. Monorail. Monorail.' No one else is on it though; it's deserted. And, although poised, Jimmy doesn't get any decent photos of rusted-out factories or grand old dilapidated buildings. He doesn't get any photos of anything at all. He's getting edgy about missing out on the old industrial relics he'd imagined shooting, with the kind of light you could never recreate in Photoshop. The lap of the city on the monorail is over quickly and we head back to the diner to collect our bags. Jimmy is quiet and sullen, and books an Uber earlier than we have to.

'I feel like I've wasted my time here,' he says. 'Can we stay longer?'

'Can't,' I say, feeling guilty about bursting his bubble. 'We've got to get you across to the West Coast and I have to get back for the convention in Atlanta.'

'Yeah, I keep forgetting about that.'

The car arrives and Jimmy gets in the back with his camera on his knee, just staring at it like his bad luck is all the camera's fault. I talk to the driver, a local fella named Clayton who has a thick head of mini dreads and Kraftwerk pumping out of the stereo. I like him already. He asks us where we want to go and I can't even remember our destination before Jimmy says, 'Anything I can take a photograph of.'

Clayton asks: 'You mean like landmarks 'n' shit?' He leans over and looks at Jimmy and the camera. 'Sure, man.' He swaps Kraftwerk for The Commodores like he's officially switching into Motown mode, and drives us around all kinds of buildings and rundown parts of town, places busting with character. Jimmy's eyes light up like someone's plugged him in. These are exactly the places he's wanted to photograph for the last two days and couldn't find. He's ecstatic as he shoots left and right, and I get a sweet interview from the big man about his lowdown on freedom while we cruise.

Clayton is enjoying taking us around and talking. I point to a baseball cap on the dash with a big Detroit Tigers D on the front. He bought it yesterday, he tells me. 'You have it,' he says. He's given Jimmy his photos and now he's giving me his fucking hat! Jimmy is giggling from behind his camera. The taxi driver practically mugged us last night, left us high and dry in a bad neighbourhood. Clayton went out of his way to make sure we remember Detroit fondly. I'm glad I wasn't too consumed with resentment to trust another driver.

Clayton drops us off at the Greyhound terminal, easy like Sunday morning.

Chapter Five

'I want to drive but I've also grown loyal to the silver dog,' says Jimmy. 'I feel like every bus ride now is a tribute to Milton, and the drivers from the diner. But we should get some overnighters, we're burning all our daylight with the travel. Saves on accommodation too.' He's right. If we're not behind the wheel ourselves we may as well be sleeping while someone else is.

'Where are we staying in Chicago?' I ask, having done zero recon whatsoever. Actually I wasn't even planning on stopping there at all. The purists will be livid I didn't follow Sal's every movement in Chicago and do everything he did but this is six years' worth of trips crammed into six weeks. Creative freedom through intense constraint, like Hendrix and his six-string prison cell. Jimmy pulls up a place on a cheap hotel website that looks good enough from the pictures, so we book it. We've been taken care of so far, so how bad could it be?

Really bad, as it turns out. Jimmy is silent as he locates the keys outside what looks like a flophouse in a dimly lit and abandoned street. There are stained mattresses on bare, sinking floorboards; damp blankets slung over the couch. There are towels as promised, damp too, and stained like the mattresses. Other people must be staying here with the locked doors and mess in the kitchen and bathroom. It's awful.

I figure that as long as we get some sleep without waking to find our bags, passports or kidneys missing, we can ride it out and hope for better luck at the next stop. Jimmy, however, is not rolling over for this. He calls the booking contact but can't get through, so I convince him to just drop our stuff and go get something to eat instead. We head down West Warren to what looks like a cluster of shops that might sell some grub. There's a long line of cars, mostly black SUVs, making its way up the street to the back entrance of a stadium.

Then, like a scene from *Night of the Living Dead*, the streets go from still to frenzied as people stampede around bends and out of buildings, offering high-fives and shouting 'Blackhawks! Yeah!' In what feels like a few minutes, there are hundreds of supporters running amok in an urban zombie apocalypse. It turns out that we're in the shadow of United Center and, inside, the Chicago Blackhawks have just won the Stanley Cup, for the third time in six years.

This is too much for the already jittery Jimmy; his pace quickens and, desperate for safe harbour, he makes a beeline for what is possibly the worst pizza place in Chicago. There's no David Foster Wallace-style mountain of cheese and tomato and toppings here – it's like a bomb shelter serving warm white dough with shredded pink 'ham' scooped out of a sweaty plastic bag. I'm keen to keep looking for a better option but something has switched in Jimmy's brain. His eyes are wide and black with the thousand-yard stare, and his hackles have risen like a werewolf's. He's soaked in the celebrating crowd's heightened state by osmosis and won't respond to reason or the promise of better food somewhere else.

'You want something?' asks the pizza guy as he smashes the pie with the cutter.

'Nah, mate, we just came in to get away from the crowd, we're gonna go,' I say.

'It's a free country,' he says without looking up.

But Jimmy orders two slices and as soon as they're delivered he takes off into darkened streets with long, purposeful strides in the opposite direction of where we just came from. I wonder if this is how he always travels, but then my head starts coming up with its own answers. He's not doing enough AA. He's overdue for a meeting. He's worrying about nothing and becoming a pain in the arse.

There are two ways one can respond to what just happened: consider it good luck that you happen to be in Chicago just at the moment the city erupts in celebration, or be annoyed that you're surrounded by so many happy people. I think how you react says a lot about where you're at in your own head. In my mind at any rate.

AA's fifth step is 'Admitted to God, to ourselves and to another human being the exact nature of our wrongs.' Mine here is judgement and selfishness, even though I'm trying to stop this other guy from getting us lost. Expectations start so simply but, if left unchecked, they can become judgement and resentment. And these don't go away on their own like they do with so-called 'normal' people. Sal's path to the elusive enlightenment included sin and confession like Steps Four and Five, but he doesn't do anything with the knowledge he gains. He doesn't look for his mistakes and identify his own defects of character, his shortcomings. Right now I'm not doing that either.

Sal can go moan for man, but you have to start by moaning for yourself at some stage. Like my sponsor says, 'If I want my life to get better, then it has to start with me.' Pretty sure he ripped that off his sponsor, who ripped it from someone else. Accepting the problem lies within and so the solution is tied up with sin and confession, Catholic values and being an alcoholic. Kerouac himself had traditional values but he lived a life at odds with those values. That's something that alcoholics do that non-alcoholics can't understand: why we act in spite of ourselves and our better judgement. The desire to numb overrides everything else, unless you can unburden all the crap from the past, all those things written down in Step Four.

We write it all down, now we have to tell someone? But it's not an anonymous confessional. It's with another alcoholic. Someone who gets it. Someone who's done it. Someone with experience, not an opinion. And no amount of Hail Marys or Our Fathers will make amends. That comes later, when you're face to face with those who were harmed. But the feeling of lightness that comes with unburdening all that shit is difficult to explain, although alcoholics are self-described 'fast forgetters'.

I've twice done a big formal Step Five. All I need to do at this moment in Chicago is a tiny one to alleviate my building resentment with my travelling companion. But I don't, I just yell, 'Wrong way!' when Jimmy charges off. And he doesn't seem that fazed either, just charges in the direction I point with the same intense stare.

Kerouac had written in the original draft of *On the Road* that he 'believed in a good home ... sane and sound living ... good food, good times, work, faith and hope.' But sane and sound living is not drinking yourself to death in your forties. Belief is one thing, but as it says in the Big Book, 'Faith without works is dead.' I believe in the same things Kerouac wanted, but one thing I've learned about staying sober and sane in the rooms of AA is that it's not a program for people who need it. It's not even a program for people who want it. It's a program for people willing to do it. Generally, they're willing because they tried all the other avenues and they're still short of that sane and sound living that Kerouac believed in – the thing that became more and more elusive to him as his fame grew and his middle years approached.

We get back to our rent-a-hovel and Jimmy lets off some steam about how much he hates being in that environment, drunk people running everywhere and the general mayhem. I'd prefer he kept his shit together enough not to walk completely off the map though I don't press the issue. We take stock of

'Hey, you need some colour in those pictures.' Reggie and Lady Liberty pose together to represent the five boroughs.

Penn Station, the epicentre of travel in the city that never sleeps. Rather than follow Sal north to Bear Mountain just to turn around and come right back again, we went to Pittsburgh.

n Akron, Ohio, a line of Chevrolet grilles and pickups for sale represents th
lream of the road for some. But we were still road-shy and happy riding on th
Greyhound bus at this stage.

One day you're shiny and new, just rolling along. And next thing, your tyres ar
lat, your windows are broken and your paint has faded. That's life on the road

Some of the roads in the Motor City are scarred with neglect, like Detroit itself now that the car is no longer king.

I don't have to answer to anyone else,' says Madison from Detroit. 'Wher
'm detached from authority and kinda making up my own ... that's freedom.

'Just take us anywhere I can take a photograph,' said a despondent Jimmy as we prepared to leave Detroit. 'You mean like landmarks 'n shit?' said Clayton. Hallelujah.

'Being able to live the way I want to live, that's freedom,' said Milton, as we boarded his bus in Ohio.

If you've never driven down it before, it's still there and it's still Route 66. Don't let anyone tell you any different.

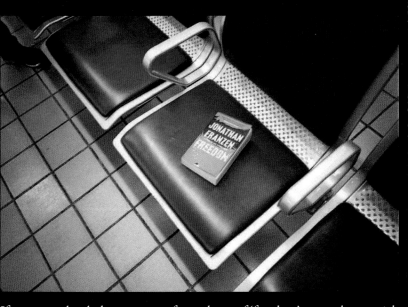

If you put a book down to pose for a photo of 'freedom', remember to pick it up again before your train comes.

Jimmy preferred to be behind the camera, like most photographers I've known. Call this his self-portrait. There certainly is freedom in anonymity.

Occasional truths among the mish-mash of San Francisco's homeless

As much as we grew to love the 'silver dog', it wasn't as free an animal as the Mustang. In the car we were no longer beholden to rigid railroad tracks and bus routes.

We drive the coast road through Big Sur, taking curves and bridges and tunnels past terrain where Kerouac hit rock bottom. Does freedom even exist on the road, or is it the state of mind you are in when you get in the car?

the slum and work out how we're going to do this. There's one lumpy bed in the room, one mattress in the main room. No obvious bedding, and no towels I'd touch without gloves. This place seems halfway between one star and dereliction. In all the excitement of the Blackhawks' 2-0 victory we also missed booking the overnight train to Omaha.

'How are we going to get out of here?'

'We could hitchhike? We're in the part where Sal got on the back of that truck with the guys travelling to the harvest.'

'Would anybody pick us up?'

'Can you be fucked carrying the bags long enough to find out?'

Hitchhiking these highways would be impossible, anyway; nobody would stop, nobody *could* stop as they hurtled along a modern highway. Even Jack admitted you couldn't thumb a ride much longer after the 50s. 'I tried, in 1960, and I couldn't get a ride. Cars going by, kids eating ice cream, people with hats with long visors driving, and, in the backseat, suits and dresses hanging. No room for a bum with a rucksack.'

As romantic a notion hitchhiking may sound, Sal only hitched from Chicago to Denver in the novel, the greater part of his first journey was on the bus, so we're not missing out after all. But the teaching imperative remained. If *On the Road*, beneath the surface, is a book about how to live your life, then the only alcoholic hitchhiker we need is Edgar, the man who hitchhiked across the country as an under-the-bridge hobo of the first order, making Kerouac and Cassady look like first-class commuters. He made it out too. He got off the road and was handed his pearl of wisdom and now he's around to pass it on to others.

I used to hitch home from high school sometimes in the 80s. Even in a school blazer and tie, people would pretend they didn't see you. As soon as I could drive, I made an effort to give people a ride where I could, even before I had a licence, and even when I wasn't exactly doing them a favour. The first car I had after I got my licence was a tiny yellow Suzuki hatchback with three cylinders of raw power under the hood and the nickname 'The Yellow Peril'. I'd smashed off the front bumper in a casino car park, leaving the fender with a sharp dent. (I put the bumper in the back and drove off, last thing you want to do is linger at a crime scene). I drove the Peril for a while before I got pulled over by a motorbike cop. He ran his finger down the fender and cut his skin, saying 'I hope your car doesn't have AIDS, mate,' as he cleaned himself up. I looked at the fender and looked at him and replied, 'I hope you don't give it to the car.' He slapped a canary, a sticker of unroadworthiness, on the windscreen in seconds. 'Get this fucking piece of shit off the road,' was the end of the conversation.

I ripped the unroadworthy sticker off and took the car on a long trip, which was as close as I ever got to Dean Moriarty driving a stolen car. On my way back to Melbourne, I picked up a hitchhiker on the outskirts of a town called Colac.

'I'm going to Melbourne,' I said.

'Yeah, I'm going that way,' he replied.

'Just so you know, I've got a ripped canary sticker,' I told him. I pointed to the top corner of the windscreen.

He just shrugged and said, 'Fine with me.'

I drove down the main street of Colac and passed an oncoming police car. I had a feeling they saw me, maybe it was that intuitive inner voice they talk about in the Big Book. I watched the police car do a U-turn in my rear-view mirror, so I immediately turned left and drove through the backstreets of town, parallel to the highway. I don't know what the hitchhiker was thinking but he didn't bat an eyelid. I came back out at the edge of town, thinking I'd shaken them off my tail. No sooner was I back on the highway than they were right up my arse, lights flashing. I pulled over and figured I'd just fess up.

'What are you running from, mate?' asked the cop in his best intimidating voice.

'Nothing, officer. I've just got a canary that's been ripped off the windscreen and I didn't want to get done driving an unroadworthy vehicle. Guess I have been, though.'

'Yeah right, mate. What are you really running from?'

'What?'

'What are you really running from? You turned off the highway pretty quick when you saw us U-turn.'

'Just the canary. That's it,' I said.

He pointed to the hitchhiker. 'Who's this?'

I looked at my passenger and looked back at the cop. 'I dunno.'

'You dunno?'

'Nup.'

'What?'

The hitchhiker helpfully said, 'He just picked me up back there, officer.'

'Get out of the car.'

I think they were annoyed at the increasing prospect that, rather than shifty criminals, we were just two fucking morons wasting their time. They made me empty out everything from the car so they could search it, questioning the hitchhiker while they did so, but when they found nothing incriminating and their questions kept getting bland, normal, honest answers, they decided I really was only worried about the car's unroadworthy status and let me go. They even let me drive it back to Melbourne. There's no way police would let you do that anymore. A few years after this, I would have lost my licence and paid a fine as expensive as the car itself.

Here in Chicago, though, there will be no hitchhiking. There's no little yellow Suzuki hatch either. There's not even an overnight train to Omaha. No jazz in Chicago clubs or kicks or 'it'. There's just two strung-out AA members on a stained mattress in a dank flophouse behind the hockey stadium.

•

Heading into the centre of Chicago on the rail, we're sure that we're nowhere near the good part of the city. We've no idea where the good part even is, but we're certain it's not here. I find a listing for a local meeting and Jimmy, surprisingly, agrees to come even though everything seems like a chore to him right now.

We turn a corner and find a few buildings and structures that seem pulled from Christopher Nolan films, and Jimmy starts taking shots with the sun straight over head. A wild-haired man perched on a chair on the sidewalk sees him and starts yelling, 'Why you taking pictures of a alley? Who the fuck take pictures of a alley? It's a alley!'

Jimmy looks at me quizzically and grins and keeps going and the wild-haired fella keeps going too. 'You never see a alley before?' he yells from his little seat on the pavement. I try to steer us toward the meeting address and take a couple of wrong turns, eventually coming out near our wild-haired mate, who is yelling at someone else now.

There are half-a-dozen people in the meeting, including us. We're the only ones sitting in the first three rows of the arc of chairs, which is not exactly inspiring. The guys here aren't interested or interesting, and it's a total waste of time.

'Man, I'm glad the meetings I go to aren't all like that,' I say.

'That was an unhappy meeting,' says Jimmy.

'How you feeling?'

'I'm glad I'm only here for one night. Those hockey fans really annoyed me, I fucking hate that environment.' Jimmy breathes out and puts his head back.

'Fair enough. The accommodation didn't help either.'

'I just want to get the fuck out of here. Where to next?'

'Omaha.'

'Have you got a contact there?'

'Yeah, this local guy, Scott. He's Annie's business mentor.'

'Is he in the rooms like Edgar?'

'No.'

'So no chance of open weeping?'

'Maybe. I've never met him. How did you find the meeting?'

'It was good to check in. I was a bit in my head. Shit meeting but, yeah, I feel better. Beats having to get pissed and then get stuck here.'

'Yes, it does. I wouldn't want to go there every week either. Shall we head back to the slum and get our stuff?'

'Yeah, let's get outta here.'

Recovering alcoholics need to work their program and that's hard to do sitting on the couch watching TV. There are no newcomers or other alcoholics to work with at home and no coworkers to become resentmentful of and no sponsor to share the resentments with. When it doesn't work out, you just have to suck it up and look for the next right thing to do and then go do it. An alcoholic who wants to stay on the right track has to practice the AA principles in all their affairs, meaning you have to have affairs to practice them in, then make mistakes or take the good times with the bad and deal with them sober. You have to act human to stay human. You have to live life on life's terms to live free.

•

The door folds closed and the bus rolls west out of Illinois. I'm talking to a 19-year-old named PJ, who's travelling from Pennsylvania to Wisconsin. All he has with him is what he's wearing and a tiny cooler bag. He's moving for a job in sales, he tells me, shoving a pinch of chewing tobacco under his lip. On the inside of his right arm is tattooed, 'Hate the sin, not the sinner.' He's flicking through Tinder profiles like he's shuffling cards and I see a bit of Dean Moriarty in him, moving through women as fast as he's moving through state lines. How would diehard *On the Road* fans feel if their sister came home with her new boyfriend and it was a grinning con man like Dean Moriarty on her arm? That's a good measure of how you really feel about another man: what you would feel if he were sleeping with your sister.

PJ moves up to another seat at the front of the bus. He had about half a seat to work with due to the passenger beside him taking up most of the area. The bus stops in the small town of La Salle for a lunch break, or cigarette stop, depending on who you are. Jimmy shoots the portrait of a wispy-haired fella with long grey sideburns and no top teeth, his face awned by a USA baseball cap. What I really want is a portrait of greasy little PJ, swiping through the girls on his phone as his Tinder beeps with alerts of willing victims in every new zip code the bus rolls through. It rolls through quite a few as we head toward Omaha. He looks to have found himself a young female companion for the rest of the ride.

It might be happening right before my eyes, the scene in *On the Road* that goes: 'I took up a conversation with a gorgeous country girl wearing a low-cut cotton blouse that displayed the beautiful sun-tan on her breast tops.' Sal begins promisingly, like PJ, but, 'She was dull. She spoke of evenings in the country making popcorn on the porch ... "And what else do you do for fun?" I tried to bring up boyfriends and sex.' Translation: I tried to get her to talk about banging me, I'm not interested in anything else. 'Her great dark eyes surveyed me with emptiness and a kind of chagrin that reached back generations and generations in her blood from not having done what was crying to be done – whatever it was, and everybody knows what it was.' Everybody = Sal. And because she won't do what he wants, she actually exercises the power of no, she must be empty inside like her dark eyes. I mean, who wouldn't want to immediately get it on with the next filthy transient they met at the bus terminal? Surely that's the wet dream of every girl with a hint of self-esteem. '"What are we all aching to do?"' he asks. 'She didn't know. She yawned. She was sleepy. It was too much. Nobody could tell. Nobody would ever tell. It was all over. She was 18 and most lovely, and lost.' It's quite a poetic way to write, 'She just didn't give a shit and it was only all about me for me, not her.'

I'm thinking about the next destination more now. How good it will be in Denver, or San Francisco. Like Sal wrote: it will be better in the next place. Like, I don't have enough time to dig where I am right now so I have to keep moving. I'd love to stop in Des Moines and sit in the diner like Sal and see if the girls are still pretty like they were 50 years ago but to get to Denver and beyond in time for Atlanta there's no time to stop.

Then the fear starts. The head chatter. 'You're not giving it enough time/doing it justice/doing it right/you're doing it wrong/you're not good enough.' It always comes back to 'not good enough': that alcoholic lack of self-esteem. The classic trait, and often the root of the whole enchilada of alcoholism. It's not just alcoholics, of course, but it does seem to be all alcoholics and it's a tight fucking rope to walk every day.

I didn't learn until I got into the rooms of AA that I had to do estimable acts (actions contrary to my regular selfish default thinking that would build my self-esteem) for that thinking to change. Fuck it, it's going to have to be good enough. When people say, 'If it's worth doing, it's worth doing badly,' they mean times like this. I'm going where I'm going in the time I have with the funds I could muster and I'll get what I'll get. If it doesn't work out, there's always self-publishing. If there's one thing alcoholics are good at, it's self.

•

Scott, my partner Annie's work contact, reaches me by phone when we hit Omaha and recommends a diner; it's the oldest in town and exactly what you want from an American diner, like the one in Detroit that offered crockery and retired Greyhound drivers. We sit at the counter and Jimmy gets stuck into the newspaper, while I start talking to John, a neatly groomed, polite and friendly guy in his forties. I'm talking to him because he's sitting next to me and, so far on the road, the person next to you is fair game for a conversation about freedom. John is an ex-Navy man so I'm particularly keen to get his take on the topic. Freedom to him means being financially stable enough to follow any career path. He's pretty adamant about this too, there was no umming and ahhing with John. It's like his response was prepared earlier: 'It's about working according to your God-given spiritual gifts as opposed to just working for safety and financial security.'

Fuck me, if this guy is living what he's saying, he must be at least halfway to living a happy life. The waitress places a plate in front of me stacked with eggs, hash browns and toast. There's bottomless coffee too for my $7 and I wonder if I've stumbled upon El Dorado in the back streets of Omaha.

I barely notice Jimmy leaving, as I ruminate on John's idea about working according to your God-given spiritual gifts. John never said what religion he is or if he follows one at all, but he seemed to have conviction in his words, and looked to me equally comfortable reading the newspaper on his own as talking to a complete stranger about something he's risked his life for.

En route to a post office, I pass a barbershop called Arlen's and head inside. Arlen has feel-good clichés pinned all over the inside of his store and no hair. I get him to clip my beard and hit him up for some material. 'Freedom is misunderstood,' he says, without missing a beat. 'It is who you are and how you behave. There's no such thing in the United States as freedom. It's in your head and your heart.'

This is that Nelson Mandela, free-in-a-jail-cell school of thought that believes freedom is a state of mind, not a state of circumstance. John in the diner was on a similar path, and both theories revolve around how you feel, rather than your external situation. Arlen's version doesn't involve having to go 'out there' to find anything; it's right there in your head and your heart, so you take it with you wherever you go anyway.

I like this idea. There's no need to run because freedom isn't out there. If you don't have the freedom in your head and your heart, then no matter where you go, you won't find it – it will remain elusive. It's like taking alcoholism everywhere and wondering why the same shit goes wrong wherever you go. This Arlen cat is on to something. Until he says, 'There's never been anyone I met who was a stranger,' and I begin to think he might be spending too much time in his shop reading his upbeat slogans.

Jimmy and I rendezvous at Wash World, in what must be Omaha's Latin quarter. The locals fold clothes and chat in Spanish while their kids swarm over the benches. We walked most of the way here and Jimmy admits he hates walking, physically having to put one foot in front of the other. This is his latest gripe, and I wonder why he agreed to travel this way with me instead of staying in New York. Maybe he didn't know he didn't like it until he tried it. I didn't know I did either.

Besides me and Jimmy, there's only one other white guy in Wash World and he looks whiter than the sheets the women are folding with his little glasses and blond jarhead cut. He talks at a news broadcast of a school shooting we're all half-watching with a shake of the head and a 'need more guns in more hands to stop shooters like that'. It doesn't occur to me to ask this guy for his take on freedom.

•

Scott calls over to where we're staying, a multi-room setup not unlike the one in Chicago, except here everything is clean, and the owner is keen to help.

Scott is a stocky fellow with a big white-toothed smile framed by a thin brown goatee, and he's very happy to meet us. He takes us to the Drover, an Omaha institution famed for steak, steak and more steak. En route, Scott says Omaha might have a name for being boring or just 'middle America', but it's a great place to work and raise a family.

'You're really free to move to a better location in this country to live your life – if you want to,' he informs us.

Inside the Drover, it's all about cow. There's even steak soaked in whiskey. This is the first steak I've had in a long time, maybe even years, and I'm looking forward to a plate full of beef. Whiskey free, of course. Jimmy's Chicago tension seems to have disappeared and he admires a huge portrait on the wall of a frontiersman in a Stetson hat with a crow's-feet smile and a cigar protruding from the corner of his mouth. I ask Scott about his political leanings and he tells me 'the truth is somewhere in the middle' – the Democrats are too far left and the Republicans are too far right. He's a homeowner with a family who works hard and gives back and just wants the freedom to do exactly that.

After we've put away a side of beef, Scott takes us on a drive around the best side of town. 'Warren Buffet, the seventh richest person in the USA, still lives here,' he says. That's pretty damn rich. Scott says he's in a modest house and regularly gives money to charity.

'It's a town of entrepreneurs,' he says, and with that puts a call through to Sebastian, who Scott tells us actually owns the house we're staying in and a few others just like it. We find Sebastian back at the house with a cooler full of beers. He's gone through a few by the time we arrive, keen to espouse his ideas on freedom. I don't take notes.

Although Scott reassured us that there's more than meets the eye here in Omaha, we decide to skip town, and I back Jimmy's idea of booking the overnight train to Denver. I had no idea before we got here that the closer you get to the departure date, the higher the price of the tickets. It's a pain in the arse and I'm soon cursing our spontaneity. If Dean Moriarty were to show up in a Hudson, I'd likely get in.

The Amtrak departure lounge is a swinging 70s pad, minus the fondue, drugs, girls, orange lampshades and actual swing. It's basically brown – not even mission brown, just a kind of drab, paper-bag brown – and I love it. I go to capture its timeless lethargy on film but the clerk, Colonel Sanders' less successful younger brother, yells, 'No photos.' He's not joking either. And this is definitely his house – what he says goes. Fuck's sake.

I board the train covered from head to toe like I'm off to scale a snowy mountain – good job too, because the Amtrak AC is set to fucking freezing again. But I'm snug in my layers as the carriages clack slowly along and the city lights drop off.

I wake to a fiery ball on the horizon, not knowing if we're up on the Colorado plateau or over the Nebraska flatlands and I like it that way – not knowing, I mean. Kerouac wrote about the surrounds, though, like they would be missed by the highway travel: '... no one will get sentimental or poetic any more about trains and dew on fences at dawn in Missouri.' Inspiring youth rebellion is one thing, but *On the Road*, for all the drunken mayhem, does spark a want for natural American scenery. The lush greens of Pennsylvania, crossing the rivers of Ohio and the smokestacks of Cleveland manufacturing, they're all still here and they make their own poetry for anyone willing to read over them.

While I slept, Tim was making plans for our visit and his friend, Dan, has messaged me. Jimmy sees me scrolling through the messages and is now used to the drill.

'Where are we staying in Denver?' he says.

'Dunno, but Tim has set us up with a local member.'

'Will there be weeping?'

'Fingers crossed. He's meeting us at the station now.'

Chapter Six

In the clear light of a Denver morning, I take a minute to find our position on a crumpled map of the USA. We're a long way west of the palatial Jersey pad and the meeting in the Village. We've passed through an Akron anniversary, had a hypo in Detroit and met an unfortunate Chicago not advertised in the brochures. Now we're in Sal and Dean's Denver, the place where it's all going to be better.

This is the first major stop in *On the Road*. Up until hitting Denver, it's been about getting here, with a little about Des Moines and Cheyenne along the way, but mostly the promise of the good times upon arrival. Up near the Rockies and the home of Dean, Sal's sideburned hero of the snowy west, Sal's finally going to get some kicks.

We're heading to a diner to meet our man Dan when we're suddenly jolted by, well, culture shock, I suppose. Everyone appears healthy and vibrant, and they're all good-looking with smiles and tanned skin. We find seats at the diner and a beautiful waitress greets us.

'Where are we?' Jimmy asks, looking around like he's just woken up.

I shrug. 'Denver.'

'Are we in the same country where we caught the train?'

A short, middle-aged fellow stops at our table and points. 'Len and Jimmy?'

His point becomes an open hand and he comes over. 'Hi, I'm Dan,' he says, shaking our hands. 'It's good to see you guys.'

Dan has popped out from work to take us to his place where we'll stay for the weekend. As we drive, Dan offers us his wife's car because she's away for the weekend. His phone keeps beeping but he seems totally unruffled and unrushed. He tells me interesting places to go and Jimmy great places to shoot, and *then* he offers his chalet in the mountains if we want to go snowboarding!

'You're a snowboarder?' asks Jimmy.

'Oh yeah, man, I only got into it a coupla years ago but I love it. I love it so much I bought a little house up there.'

Jimmy sits back into his seat, then launches forward to ask, 'Dan, how old are you?'

'Oh, I'm as old as I look. Even though I stopped heroin years ago. But I feel young. Hey, we're here.'

Jimmy doesn't get time to follow up before Dan is showing us the security lock to his house and apologising that he has to head back to work.

'Hey, Dan, look, are you sure you're okay just leaving us here with all your stuff?'

'Yeah, sure. Why, what are you going to do? Take my house back to Australia? Tim said you guys were all right, so don't worry about it. I'll call you later, see how you're doing.'

We don't make the most of this generosity. In fact, the first time we try to take Dan's wife's car for a spin, we struggle so much with the manual transmission that we drive it back and get an Uber downtown. With our equilibrium partly restored, we head toward Sal's old stomping ground, Larimer Street. I duck into a café for a takeaway coffee and spy a poster above the bar with Jack Kerouac's face plastered on it. At various points around Larimer Street and downtown Denver, someone has stenciled pictures of Kerouac, Banksy style, with lines from *On the Road* and other material. 'Jack was here' has been sprayed on the wall outside, although it's a neat and tidy alley and not quite the haven for the drunken transients of Sal's time.

Nearby is a 'Green Cross', an over-the-counter weed store, prevalent in Denver now that cannabis has been legalised. Legal weed? The Beat artists would love this. It seems Colorado might have an idea about this freedom thing and it certainly doesn't appear to be having a negative impact on the place; in fact, Denver feels positively salubrious compared to everywhere else we've been so far. Jimmy isn't keen on heading into the old environment but I can't resist and have to at least have a look.

Inside the weed den, for this is what I'm imagining, I'm a bit disappointed to see that it's just like a regular bar. Instead of single malts and beers, there's a selection of strains and hybrids. They have edible and smokeable weed and the selection comes in what looks like old photographic film canisters, which really might have sent Jimmy over the edge, and each smells like it would get you nicely toasted.

The 'bartender' tells me he was considering moving to another country entirely before the law was passed to decriminalise and legalise the sale and consumption of pot in Colorado. He believes the Green Cross and places similar are a step in the right direction for American freedom. From the look of all the vibrant, healthy-looking people who greeted us at Union Station, it doesn't seem to be doing the place any harm. 'People in Denver, they like to go outside and they like to get high,' the seller informs me. Mile High City indeed.

This isn't what I imagined back when I was a participant, but it reminds me of harvesting a hydroponic setup when I was younger, living in a place that had a jungle of the stuff growing in a granny flat. The air in there was so dense with vapour that we got high just harvesting and bagging the plants in the summer heat, something I didn't think was actually possible until the giggling kicked in. Still remember carrying the bags out into the street in broad daylight to shove them in the boot of a car wearing nothing but a pair of shorts – and sunglasses so nobody would recognise me, of course.

Kerouac walked these streets and wrote about them a ton but they're not like they were in the late 40s. Although that is partly due to Kerouac himself and how he viewed the world, as a writer and, in my opinion, as an alcoholic. 'At lilac evening I walked with every muscle aching among the lights of 27th and Welton in the Denver colored section, wishing I were a Negro, feeling that the best the white world had offered was not enough ecstasy for me, not enough life, joy, kicks, darkness, music, not enough night.' I remember all the times when there was not enough night for me and the 'white' world was the world of going to bed early, getting up and going to work and – unbeknown to me at the time – accepting life's responsibilities. I yearned for more of the night and the darkness not because it had more kicks so much as it was further away from the world I didn't understand how to live in. I've been out drunk and made friends with other people who were out in the night just so that I didn't have to drink alone. If I was in Denver or anywhere in Kerouac's time, I'd be wanting to drink with the people I found and I would wish I was one of them just as he did. One of the genuine underclass, instead of an alcoholic tourist longing to be something he's not.

In the time of Kerouac and Cassady's road trips, no one was as beholden to an underclass life as the coloured folks. It's not like Jack had some genuine affinity for the black population either. He talks about jazz like it's jungle drums and tribal rhythms instead of skilled musicianship that takes years of sweat and toil to master, and there isn't a passage where Sal and Dean are particularly interested in any black people beyond booze, drugs or sex. For Sal, the whole point was about being anyone except himself: 'I wished I were a Denver Mexican, or even a poor overworked Jap, anything but what I was so drearily, a "white man" disillusioned.'

For Sal and Dean, it isn't really about race or colour or culture; it's that alcoholic dream of being someone else, anyone else, so you don't need to look at yourself and do anything about your behaviour. It's self-loathing. In his journals, Kerouac wrote, 'Some people are just made to wish they were other than what they are, only so they may wish and wish and wish. This is my star.' Spoken like a true alcoholic. Big ego, low self-esteem, translated as: 'I think I'm a piece of shit, but I'm all I think about.' *On the Road*'s compass points in no clear direction because it doesn't have one. Escaping from yourself means perpetual running. No matter where you go, there you are, so you're stuck, whether you're on the road or not.

For an alcoholic, the drinking lets you be that someone else and mix with those you'd rather be for a time. Then you sober up and feel the pain of reality more and more – a '"white man" disillusioned'. The problem with alcoholic drinking is after a while it stops working and the damage the drinking is doing supersedes the pain relief. But you can't *not* drink either; the accumulated pain of day-to-day living just gets more intense. It doesn't just roll off your back like it does for 'regular' people. So you have to up the ante. Becoming a regular at the Green Cross might work for a while but alcoholism is a disease of more – more of whatever relieves the pain. As I've said, we're comfort junkies at heart.

From the antics of *On the Road*, Sal seems to have done what I and many others I know did for years: look for some kind of authenticity and relief from disillusionment by just trying to control everything that is 'out there', like an actor trying to arrange the entire production. But in my experience, and the experience of others I know, authenticity is revealed – it is already inside, under the layers of self. Under the resentments, the harm, the fears, the lies, the fronts, the myths, and the bullshit: the character defects that Step Six talks about asking God to remove. Sounds easy enough – if you're willing to admit that the problem might not be everyone and everything else, and it might not even be the booze itself.

'This "Jack lives here" stuff is just a few shit stencils that some hipster's put all over the place,' says Jimmy. He's on the rant and it's solid.

'This is bullshit. I'm not photographing any of it.' He's taking a small but, for him, significant stand.

'Yeah, you're right. It's not showing us much. I think it's just a homage.'

'We'd be better off going with Dan up to his snowboarding hut. Or hitting the weights in his man cave.'

We walk through clean streets full of happy people, breathing crisp air in warm sunshine. Sal's down-and-out

Denver seems Byzantine in comparison. To us, the city is the epitome of clean living, Green Cross and all. We stop to check our itinerary.

'I've decided to go home a couple of days early,' Jimmy says.

'Oh,' I say casually, 'okay.'

We barely miss a beat, just carry on as if nothing has changed, but it has. Jimmy wouldn't admit it, but I wonder if skipping Las Vegas and all it represents is part of his reason to bail out early.

'Hey, mate, why did you say you wanted to go to Vegas in the first place?'

'I dunno. I just thought that's where you're supposed to go here to have a good time.' He's doing that hands-in-pockets, staring-ahead move like in Chicago.

'Yeah, but chopping days off now is a bit of a pain in the arse.'

'I'm just not interested in going there now. It'll be like that night in Chicago but on fucking steroids.'

'Then why did you say you wanted to go there for your birthday and leave from there?'

'Because I didn't fucking know. Now I know, I don't want to go. I hate going to the pub in sobriety so I don't go. Vegas is just a big fucking pub in the middle of the desert.'

And he's right – it sounded great in theory, but all the excess on tap is what got Jimmy in the shit in the first place. The Vegas dream isn't necessarily the Vegas reality and somewhere in Colorado, Jimmy had a moment of clarity. You can't stay annoyed with someone for just trying to protect themselves.

'You're leaving, remember, I've still got a few weeks here and I'm doing it on a shoestring, I can't just drop cash on flights and move shit around – I'm lining up couches to stay on as it is.'

Jimmy doesn't say anything until his phone lights up and he takes a call from Dan, who asks us if we want to go to the Saturday night meeting in Boulder and grab dinner with friends of his. Much to my surprise, Jimmy jumps at the chance. Back at the house, he heads for the man cave to book his flight home from Los Angeles and I look for a suitable vehicle to pick up from San Francisco. We're going to have to fly to San Francisco now to go from there to LA for his flight and as much as I had wanted to stop in Salt Lake City and get the Mormon take on freedom, it's not going to happen.

Dan soon returns and takes a few minutes to meditate before we all pile into his car for the 40-minute drive to Boulder.

Jimmy taps me on the shoulder. 'Did you find any cars?'

'Yeah, there's a few deals, can pickup from the airport pretty easily.'

'Wanna go halves in a decent one?'

'Yeah. All right.'

Jimmy asks Dan about his meditation practice.

'I love it,' says Dan. 'Meditation allows us to slow down our thinking. All our negativity and dishonesty, the problem centres in our mind. Meditation allows me to see that there's something else besides my thinking, you know? There's something else underneath all my crap.' Dan's phone beeps but he barely looks at it. 'I practise morning and afternoon, just a few minutes between work and snowboarding and hanging out with Helen. Sometimes you've just gotta sit still and realise that under all the character defects, we're all just human, but that's okay. That's all we're supposed to be. I never really got there back in the days we were all taking acid and drinking bottles of whiskey.'

In *On the Road*, Sal and the others briefly leave for a mountain trek out of Denver and into the Rockies. While tonight's meeting in Boulder isn't quite mountaineering on foot with a skin full, 'Saturday Night Jive' is a welcome little detour. It's a speaker meeting, where a selected member talks for about 20 minutes on their experience. Tonight's guy is six foot tall with a shaved head and collar all buttoned up to the throat like a British football hooligan. He talks about having a 'normal' girlfriend who has one or two drinks, and then he stops abruptly. 'What the fuck is with that? That's the best part! You don't stop because you're getting drunk, you keep drinking!' he says, and ripples of laughter go through the crowd. He talks about being free of his own crap just enough, every day, to stay in a healthy relationship, adding this is the greatest gift he's received since joining AA. The meeting winds up after a few other speakers and we head into the main street. I find a first edition of *Serenade* by James M. Cain in a second-hand bookstore while Dan and a few others are watching the buskers from a communal bench.

Jimmy nudges me and points at Dan. 'Look at this guy,' he says. 'Not a fucking care in the world. Did you hear what he said about his meditation?'

'Yeah. He's pretty relaxed.'

'Relaxed? He's in the moment. All the time. He's got *it*.'

'It?'

'It.'

'What?'

'It. That's his vibe. I don't know what it is, but he's got it.'

When they're talking about 'it' in *On the Road*, it goes: '"Now, man, that alto man last night had IT ... Ah well" – Dean laughed – "now you're asking me impon-de-rables – ahem! Here's a guy and everybody's there, right? Up to him to put down what's on everybody's mind. He starts the first chorus, then lines up his ideas, people, yeah, yeah, but get it, and then he rises to his fate and has to blow equal to it. All of a sudden somewhere in the middle of the chorus he gets it – everybody looks up and knows: they listen; he picks it up and carries. Time stops. He's filling empty space with the substance of our lives, confessions of his bellybottom strain, remembrance of ideas, rehashes of old blowing."'

Jimmy is talking about something similar, but bigger. It's not about the meditating and the meetings. It is effortlessly enjoyable normality, joy in the mundane. The freedom to be in the moment. Dan's a former alcoholic, heroin-hitting acid tripper who's now a middle-aged snowboarder with hospitality beyond measure who can handle a job and a long-term relationship. His alarm goes off again, and I'm finally pressed into enquiry.

'How come your phone keeps going off non-stop?'

'Oh, it's just a reminder alert.'

'Of what?' asks Jimmy.

'That it's God's will, not mine. I just need to be reminded.' He pauses. 'Say, you guys are flying out, right?'

'Yeah, we booked the flights just before,' I say.

'Helen will drive you to the airport, no worries. She's back at the house now, she just sent me a message. It's a shame you guys can't stay longer.'

'Yeah, it is,' says Jimmy. 'I'd love to stay here a bit longer. Hey, Dan, would it be all right if I came back with my girlfriend next year?'

'Sure, we'd love to have you over. You can stay at our place up in the mountains.'

'I enjoyed that meeting, by the way, thanks for taking us out there.'

'No problem.'

Jimmy looks at me and nods. 'Man cave,' he says.

•

'We hated each other when we first met,' Helen says about her and Dan. 'Now he's my favourite person.'

Helen is little and full of life, like Dan, and similarly easygoing. 'We met in the rooms and got together and had a hell of a time at the start.'

'Why was that?' I ask.

'Well, you know, it's just hard. We're selfish people by nature. Our pride is easily hurt – and there's loads of it. We clashed over little things because neither of us had any idea how to compromise or even communicate.' She flicks her fingers from the steering wheel as she talks. 'It took a long time to calmly say to Dan what I needed instead of demanding it like a kid. Him too,' she says with a smile. 'We were like angry teenagers in adult bodies. Everything we learned about relationships we've learned from each other and that means making mistakes and forgiving. Even when I'm being a bitch and he's being a bastard!'

I love her sass and Jimmy is hanging on her every word. I can't help thinking that if we'd met Dan and Helen earlier, Jimmy wouldn't be quitting the trip early.

Helen makes their relationship sound like what Dean and Camille's could have been if Dean didn't run when it got to the point of pain, or if they grew through the behaviour of angry tantrum-throwing children. Carolyn Cassady, the real life Camille, wrote after Neal Cassady's death, 'He is known to have hit women, but I'm sure they asked for it, and that it was a sexual turn-on, as some have confessed to me.' Kerouac wrote it a little differently: 'Marylou was black and blue from a fight with Dean about something; his face was scratched. It was time to go.' The confrontation; the departure. Not growing emotionally and relying on angry lashing out to secure an outcome is a classic symptom of alcoholism and addiction. Many alcoholics in recovery will tell you they can pinpoint the beginning of their drinking to the beginning of adolescent feelings and emotions and an inability to handle them, not that they put two and two together at the time. But dulling it with drinking and other gratifying behaviours never allows one to learn how to articulate emotions, discern between facts and feelings, and respond to the world, instead of simply reacting.

Dan and Helen, former hard-core alcoholic drug addicts, seem like they couldn't be further from domestic violence, but Helen assured me she and Dan hated each other for the first year they were together, until they learned how to actually stay in, grow through and develop an adult relationship.

According to Carolyn Cassady, what Kerouac missed when he wrote Neal as Dean Moriarty the hero was that Neal was desperately trying to change. But how do you stay motivated to change when you're put up on a saintly pedestal? Approval of others isn't exactly the kind of pain that is a touchstone to spiritual growth. According to Sal, Dean is the Holy Goof. It's like nothing is his responsibility, so until you're willing to accept responsibility for your shortcomings and change within, nothing will be different without.

From my experience of recovery through a twelve-step program, Step Six gets one conscious of these character defects and the selfishness that comes with them, in preparation for asking something else to remove them, awakening the spirit as the self gets out of the way: 'We're entirely ready to have God remove all these defects of character.' It's a state of mind for when all the crap from the personal inventory has been purged with writing it down and sharing it with another. You're ready to let go of your own bullshit. Unless, of course, your own bullshit is too dear to part with.

Galatea Dunkel really nailed it in one passage from *On the Road*. '"Dean, why do you act so foolish? ... You have absolutely no regard for anybody but yourself and your damned kicks. All you think about is what's hanging between your legs and how much money or fun you can get out of people and then you just throw them aside."' She sums up most people's AA drinking story in a few sentences and she is the only one with the guts to tell the truth. But that's not what the women are for in *On the Road*. The women are used as agents to validate the 'sin' (Cassady and Kerouac are, after all, Catholic boys with Catholic guilt). And, by offering domestic boredom, the women make running the far better option. But Dan and Helen stayed and grew through the times that made guys like Sal and Dean hit the road. Now they share the road with each other. They are each other's favoured travelling companion.

Except for Marylou, who is identified from the start as 'dumb and capable of doing horrible things', women rarely join Sal and Dean on the road. There's the passage about the girl in Denver where Sal says, 'I wanted to go and get Rita again and tell her a lot more things, and really make love to her this time, and calm her fears about men.' More like Sal looking to calm his own fears about himself. Dean 'found' Rita for Sal in Denver, a 'fine chick, slightly hung-up on a few sexual difficulties which I've tried to straighten up and I think you can manage, you fine gone daddy you.' Translation: 'I've done her, she was crap, but she will do for your sorry, glum, alcoholic arse.' Said in the friendliest possible way.

If you have low self-esteem, having another person desire you is possibly the quickest way to feel like you're worth something. But that's all you end up being worth. Worse still, like in Sal's case, he perceives his worth as having the same quality of the rest of his life – his writing, his friendships, his travels on the road, are never ever good enough. Even when talking about the ideal woman, he ends up describing a woman who is capable of 'Rushing off to mad bars, yet at the same time a sunny housekeeper.' He reminds me of the conversation in Bukowski's *Factotum*, where Bukowski's characters discuss this same dilemma, although by the end even they decide they don't want the kind of woman who would do all the things they want to do.

Missing from all these, though, is any scope for growth. If the women are not perfectly fitting into a preconceived mould, they fall short of expectations every time and all relationships ultimately fail. Dan and Helen are testament to working beyond the expectations and resentments, the pride and the selfishness. They're in a place Sal seemed to want to reach but he never found it. Dan and Helen, though, they have it. They keep on giving too. It's no coincidence that people who give always seem to have something to give and people who only take, well, they never seem to have anything.

•

There's uncharacteristic effusiveness in our thanks to Helen, and we're keen for her to thank Dan again for the hospitality although we've already thanked him a hundred times.

'Wait,' says Helen, gently grabbing my forearm and handing me a piece of paper. 'Dan wanted me to give you this.'

Inside the terminal it soon becomes apparent that I have completely fucked up the check-in time and we have missed our flight to San Francisco.

'No problem,' says Jimmy. 'I thought we should have arrived a bit earlier but these things happen.'

I stare at him in disbelief.

'We'll just get the next one,' he says. 'We'll get you to Atlanta on time, mate, and I'm sure it'll be everything you're hoping for.' He even waits patiently as I get the full-body pat down as a result of leaving my passport in my backpack, which has been stowed on the plane after the new check-in.

Thin wisps of cloud float by in high altitude air currents, mist settling in over the mountains far below, somewhere in the desert between Denver and San Francisco. The God Sal was searching for is about as much out there as it is in here. As it is in the meetings and as it was in the car with Sal and Dean. It's the crap Dan talked about that gets in our way. A connection with the world is everyone's; the defects that stop it are our own. The fault lies in ourselves, not the stars, like the Bard said many, many years ago: the resentments, the anger and the selfishness, but most of all, the fear. At some point you have to cross the divide and set aside the things that keep you shackled.

Jimmy is already buried in a book so I unfold the paper Helen gave to us.

> When I was drinking, my idea of Freedom was enough money to do what I wanted, where I wanted, and with whom I wanted. This money I was going to make would allow me to acquire those things that I equated with Freedom: Power and Control, Security, Affection, Esteem, Approval, Pleasure. Me, My, Mine. At first I used alcohol as an ally to fuel my quest for that Money/Freedom. Later, alcohol robbed me of the very symbols of freedom I had begun to acquire. That included the loss of freedom to choose when I'd get up, go out, eat meals, who I was allowed to associate with, this loss of freedom being the result of being thrown in jail for my drunken behavior. Eventually, I'd had enough of this brand of Freedom.
>
> Great good fortune and exquisite timing placed me together with a grade school friend at the nadir of my, so-called, drinking career. He recommended

that if I was looking for a way out of the mess my life had become, I should give Alcoholics Anonymous a try. He said it had worked for him and might work for me. I attended my first AA meeting in Victoria, Texas in September 1984. There I was told they had a plan (the 12 Steps), which would allow me to have 'deep and effective spiritual experiences', that I would be 'rocketed into the fourth dimension of existence' and that I would be set on the 'highroad to a new freedom.' All I had to do was practice the 12 Steps, have a spiritual awakening, then spend the rest of my life giving away the freedom I had found as the result of this new way of life.

AA's Path to Freedom has been a process of deflating my ego though the practice of the 12 Steps, leading to the gradual destruction of self-centeredness (for me, this has been, and is, an on-going process, as well as an occasional event). And so, at 32 years of sobriety, that prayer from the book Alcoholics Anonymous, which implores: 'relieve me of the bondage of self' takes on a new and deeper meaning. The less I think of me, the freer I am. AA has taught me to seek God's strength and inspiration so that I might help others meet their needs, and find their freedom, thus finding my own freedom in the process.

In the dictionary there are two very different definitions of Spirit: 'Non-flavored alcohol of 190 proof, used for blending with straight whiskeys and in the making of gin, cordials, etc.' (Collins English Dictionary – Complete and Unabridged, 12th Edition) and 'Having a relationship based on a profound level of mental or emotional communion' (Oxford Living Dictionaries).

It turns out, I have always been searching for my freedom in Spirit, and for me, true freedom is living in conscious contact with [the] Spirit of the Universe, knowing that I am guided by that Spirit, who's [sic] desire is for me to be Happy, Joyous and Free.

Jimmy's phone beeps an alert. He looks up from his book and gazes out the window for a moment, lightly nodding. Then he sticks his headphones in his ears and goes back to his book.

Chapter Seven

I wake early and head straight out toward San Francisco's Market Street, past the Adobe and Twitter offices and the people pounding the pavement on their way to work. There are also plenty of lively folk out who don't seem to be in a hurry to get anywhere but in my face. The assault soon dissipates as the street opens out to the harbour area, the wooded decks under blue sky, away from the hills; this is the San Francisco I'd imagined from all those cop shows and movies.

There are a few bums greeting the morning, huddled in a makeshift shelter as tourists stroll around taking snapshots. An old Asian man is pulling fish out of the water with a long fishing pole and I can't say why it is that wherever there's a harbour, old Asian fishermen are the ones actually catching the fish. A couple of beat cops pass by the shanty tent and stop to talk to the guys there, then leave them be and slowly make their way around the pier. Vessels from catamarans to ferries to one huge container ship all move in slow motion. A girl swaps from talking on her phone to taking pictures and back again. I offer to take her picture with the bridge and buildings in the background. I take a couple of snaps for her and she thanks me and wanders off, talking into her phone again. No clouds, no wind, just bright blue sky in all directions.

A couple of ramshackle fellas with bags of grimy clothes are sitting close to the water's edge and one pulls out a bottle of booze, throwing his head back and taking a big swig before handing it to his companion. It's mid-morning on a Tuesday and their day looks like it's starting how the last one ended. Their fingers are rusty coloured, like the facial hair under their noses, and one of them is wearing a pair of sandals on feet like bloated sweet potatoes protruding out from his pants. This must be what Edgar looked like when he was drinking. No glamour on the road any more – the road stops at the harbour and you make camp. These two fellas could be Sal and Dean in middle age, if Sal and Dean ever made it that far. I've heard some argue that there is freedom in homelessness, but drinking in the morning like this, with sores on your orange feet and rags for clothes, doesn't exactly portray a sense of liberty to me. The only time I drank so early was coming off a drug bender or at the end of my drinking days when I was scared of living life. Time to get off this dock – there's no freedom in that bottle they're passing around, only a temporary escape from it.

Around the streets where Jimmy and I are staying, there are young men in all-black garb who aggressively approach us asking for money, reeking of weed. We've seen and met some fingerless-gloved hobos in New York and Chicago but they're different here, younger. Among them moves a guy about my age wearing a lanyard and talking to some of the homeless kids while telling others, in no uncertain terms, to move on from the doorways and shopfronts. I walk with him for a minute and ask him his name and what his job is; when he picks up on my accent he stops to talk.

His name is Eric and he's a community service officer. 'San Francisco is pretty welcoming,' he says. 'But look around. This is a mess.' He points to a cluster of whippet-thin young guys in skinny black denim and black shirts. 'Some of them are fleeing bad situations, but others are just, you know, here. I think it's the sense of community – but it doesn't help them, it just enables them to keep doing what they're doing.'

Eric came down from Seattle and took this job purely because he needed one. He tells me he can't do it for much longer. 'You spend your time with people at their worst who see you as some kind of enemy. I'm not a cop, I don't arrest anyone, but it's like there are slummers' rights here that are gospel, regardless of if you've just wandered in with a drug habit and want to get away from people that know you.'

We're not in the same town of the cheap-housing rush and hippy movement that ended half-a-century ago either. Tom Wolfe might have written *The Electric Kool-Aid Acid Test* with the Merry Pranksters and Ken Kesey's psychedelic bus ride – complete with Neal Cassady at the wheel – spiking the dispensers with 'Purple Haze', but that book came out in 1968. It's history now. Sal got completely lost in a romantic myth of poverty that's history now too, like the down-and-out Larimer Street of his time in Denver. It's over, but that doesn't deter the many people trying it on in San Francisco today.

I don't know how different I was when I was drinking. I would always look for the people who drank like I did, anywhere from work functions to random people in bars, and I would always find them. I had no time for anyone else. Even though I was killing myself, it was a better option than doing it alone. But when it came to a point where I'd stopped being able to work and had no income of any kind, I was terrified of becoming homeless. To me that represented death, not Sal's ascetic lifestyle. Destitution was never about journeying beyond the comfort zone to confront aspects of yourself and examine your life, or to explore the world beyond your boundaries. As much as that goes with alcoholics and drug addicts, I've done far more of that kind of living as a sober man. Living a bum's life as an ideology – transient tourism for those who can't connect – seems more of a last-ditch attempt at belonging in the world, even if it's a death sentence.

Coming back from the harbour, a guy wearing wrestler's-style knee pads and a backward cap is ranting at pedestrians, pointing into a book and shaking his head. He reminds me of Hyman Solomon, the Jewish hitchhiker in Virginia from *On the Road*. When Sal and Dean ask what he's reading he doesn't know: 'He didn't bother to look at the title page. He was only looking at the words, as though he had found the real Torah where it belonged, in the wilderness.' Exactly what this guy was doing, right in front of me, 50 years later. There's no Torah here, though. There never was. It's mental illness unchecked. He even fits the description: 'incredibly filthy and covered in scabs ... knocking and sometimes kicking at Jewish doors and demanding money: "Give me money to eat, I am a Jew."' Unlike Hyman, this guy doesn't proclaim a faith, he just gets up in the grill of passers-by and demands money without so much as a good story for how he might spend it.

I get back to the hotel and find Jimmy has just experienced the same thing, but on a bigger scale.

'This place is fucked!' he says, with that look from Chicago.

'Where did you go?'

'Haight-Ashbury.'

'What's there?'

'Fucking nothing! Just more of those dope smokers. They're so aggressive,' he says, shaking his head. 'They're a blight on the city.'

We talk to a local guy in a restaurant later in the day who tells us vagrancy is sacred in this town. 'There's a lot of history here,' he says, talking about the hippy movement that once flourished. But it's not here anymore, it's been replaced by 20-somethings who look like they could leave at any time and go home to their parents, back in their real hometowns. But you can't call them phoneys, it's bad form – they're St Paul's Holy Fools. The Holy Goofs. And they're welcomed in this town with open arms, even if it doesn't seem to be doing any of them any favours. San Francisco was always welcoming, generous and compassionate; the homeless and vagrants flocked here to make it their new home, but it seems like it's gone too far. It's like a place to slum in safety and acceptance for those who, on face value, don't need to; perhaps they're inspired by their Beat predecessors to find some kind of pearl in a transient lifestyle. It must be second nature to locals, but Jimmy and I are hating it.

The holiness placed on Dean Moriarty neatly absolved him of all responsibility for being a drug-fuelled, women-beating liar, cheat and thief. Kerouac heaps more absolution on him the worse he behaves. That way, Kerouac never had to really look at himself. The worse he gets, like Dean, the closer to God they proclaim they are in their deluded little universe. If they suddenly saw the whole country like an open oyster, if the pearl was really there, why didn't anything change? Why did they never grow up and instead just keep drinking and die young?

Jimmy snaps some photos of the street signs and the buildings and notices we're heading back up the hill toward the area he affectionately refers as 'Hate-Ashbury'.

'What do you reckon is down this way?' he asks, pointing to a sign reading 'Castro Street'.

'I dunno, maybe Cubans?'

'Wouldn't be surprised in the slightest,' he says, clicking away. In minutes we're on Market Street, which is adorned by rainbow flags on either side.

'Um, I don't think this is the Cuban quarter,' I tell him. On the other side of the road with a huge rainbow flag is Harvey Milk Plaza, named after the first openly gay American to be elected to public office.

'Did we just walk into Darlinghurst?'

'Maybe. Fair chance of good coffee here, though.'

'Hold my hand?'

'Fuck off.'

We head into a café and order among a throng of smiling same-sex couples.

'There must be a pride march on today or something,' Jimmy says, noting the volume of rainbow flags being flown and even carried.

'Didn't you guys hear?' asks the barista.

'Hear what?'

'Check it out. Gay marriage is legal across the country now,' he states proudly. He nudges a newspaper across the counter toward us.

It's folded to display an article outlining a US Supreme Court ruling that declared attempts by conservative states to ban same-sex marriage unconstitutional. 'Can't do that in Australia,' I say to Jimmy. 'That's a freedom we haven't got.'

'I think there's more rights, though,' Jimmy says.

'Well, you two could just get married here and enjoy your rights Down Under,' the barista says with a wink, passing Jimmy his tea.

'Do you know much about Harvey Milk Plaza over there?' I ask.

'No, but I was here when Obama gave him his medal.'

'What medal? Didn't he die years ago?'

'It was awarded posthumously. They gave Harvey the Presidential Medal of Freedom.'

Same thing happened to Martin Luther King Jnr; maybe you have to be assassinated here for the majority to recognise you as a champion of freedom and civil liberty.

'Would you say this is a free country?' I ask him.

'Oh, yeah! But not everywhere all of the time.'

'What do you mean?'

'I'm free here but look around.' He gestures toward the window. 'I live in Gay Town USA. You think you'd get this in Alabama?'

The flags dissipate as we walk back along Market Street through the mission.

'That guy was right about there being a lot of history here.'

'Yeah, that's true,' says Jimmy. 'I forget we're still in the same country, you know? It's like we passed through a few different ones with no border crossings.'

'What do you wanna do?'

'Tacos?'

'Tacos.'

The next day I head out early for the Golden Gate Bridge. It looks great – no fog today, the enormous arches surreal as they tower above the ocean. There's a woman with a small trestle table at the foot of the bridge handing out pamphlets encouraging people not to jump off. But there's nothing really stopping anyone from ending it all here – the pedestrian walkway barrier fence is only waist high for the entire length of the bridge, so anyone could just hop over the side and end it if they wanted to. It really is a free country.

I walk back along the foreshore, stopping at an exercise station on the bike path with a view straight out to Alcatraz Island. Seems fitting to use the chin-up bar facing the old island prison. There's another guy here who has the same idea and we take turns on the equipment. Besides death and institutions, prison is one of the common destinations for an active alcoholic. But like an alcohol or drug related celebrity incident, doing time somehow gets associated with authenticity or originality when it comes to artists like musicians or writers having stints behind bars. Prison is about as much a prerequisite for creative originality as alcoholism, and that kind of thinking just buys into the myth that great works come from punitive suffering, not in spite of it. I once met an ex-gangster from LA who wrote a book about getting sober while attending meetings in prison. It's the sober part he writes about – making a change. If it wasn't for that, he would have remained a prisoner and written nothing. Although I've been to jail and am writing, I only ever visited as a sober AA member.

Alcoholics Anonymous runs itself, free from any funding from government or religious bodies. All the jobs, from locating venues for meetings, opening them on the night, bringing supplies and putting the chairs out are done by the members. They call these jobs 'service commitments'. They're great, because they require selfish, lazy alcoholics like me to show up regularly and do something for someone else without having to get something for it. One of the service commitments I had in my first few years of getting sober was facilitating an AA meeting in a remand prison on Saturday mornings. The meetings were popular and we soon had a regular attendance of about 20 prisoners. And then we stopped supplying coffee, sugar and tea and the attendance dropped to three. But those three were the real deal. One was a gambler on the outside and AA's Twelve Step process helped him overcome that, the other two kept coming to the meetings for the rest of the time I was on the roster. I never thought much about them to be honest, as I was doing it for me.

Some years after that I was in a daytime meeting in the city and a man came over and stood next to someone I was talking to, just grinning and bordering on psycho. 'You don't remember me, do you?' he said. I recognised his face, but couldn't pick where from besides AA in general. 'The remand centre,' he said, 'I got introduced to AA there when you used to come in and run the meeting. I'm Dave.'

Ah, Dave, one of the legit guys who kept coming after we cut out the complimentary beverages. He'd been honest and open in those meetings, honest and open when he got out, and he was now sober. Two years I went into that fucking prison to run the meeting just so they could steal coffee and sugar and I wrote them all off as phoneys. Then Dave shows up, sober and getting on with his life. It was worth it for one guy. Actually it was two guys: here was Dave, but I kept myself sober by going there too. Didn't seem to cultivate any creative genius on our parts, though.

'Being sent to prison was a paradox,' Dave told me. 'On the one hand I had lost my freedom and at times prison drove me to the point of desperation and outright despair. On the other hand, prison kept me safe from my disease of alcoholism and perdition driven by narcissistic self-will.' Dave stayed out of jail and stayed sober, undertaking degree studies after gaining his freedom. But unlike the romantic idealism of Kerouac and the creative geniuses benefitting from jail time, Dave told me, 'One problem with spending two and a half years in prison is the institutionalisation, and to this day, I still struggle with the daily tasks I need to do to function in this life.' Like Ryan in Akron, Dave left jail with the desire to live his life without having to go back to prison or drinking. A few too many beers and a night in the lock-up is one thing, but institutionalisation and a cycle of addiction and imprisonment really is a life sentence.

I walk up over the peak of a hill along the cable-car route and to the City Lights bookstore. The literary wealth generated by Lawrence Ferlinghetti's bookstore and publishing masthead is impressive; this must have really been something back in the days of Sal, Dean and Carlo Marx. Bookstores like this were performance hubs, the only places where Ginsberg could howl and those who listened could come back for more. They were hotbeds of ideas and axles for cultural shifts. Nowadays, it's still City Lights, but things are quieter on the revolutionary front. Nothing reaches out from the shelf and demands to be taken home, but what does grab my attention is a framed picture on the wall near the stairs.

It's of Neal Cassady shaving at the sink in his regular collared shirt. The caption reads that Ginsberg's place was always full of amazing people and one of them was Cassady – who didn't even like Jack Kerouac. Didn't like him? They're practically hitched as Sal and Dean in *On the Road*. But in the years following *On the Road*, Kerouac and Cassady pulled apart. Maybe it's because unattended petty resentments just grind away until the other person reminds you of all the things you hate about yourself, and pretty soon you want nothing to do with them anymore. Maybe it's par for the course when you're talking about two people living with addictions and self-centredness. But didn't like him at the time? So much for *On the Road* being the manual on bromance.

Next door to City Lights is a bar with a view overlooking the alley. The best the lanky bartender can offer me is a lemonade, but I am in a bar so I can't feel self-righteous, and pull up a stool to write some notes instead. There's a guy sitting cross-legged, European style, with hands resting atop of a cane. He's wearing a top hat, ruffled cravat and little round sunglasses, like an Alice Cooper promotional poster. He's a study of performed motionless, like a busking statue, until he removes one hand from the cane to take a sip of his stout before returning to his pose. He could have been coming to this bar in this outfit for 30 years, a relic from a bygone era. Would this be Sal now if he'd made it? Or even Dean? Entrenched in the time when you had 'it', before 'it' changed around you and left you behind. I would have liked it in here when I was drinking, no doubt. It was the kind of place I might have wanted to be known as a regular, like this guy, before being trapped in a twilight zone of my peak years while the rest of the world got on with it. I'd be largely ignored, except for the attention of the occasional judgemental writer sizing me up for some meaning on which to end a scene.

•

Jimmy is uncharacteristically spritely and ready to get moving after returning from his morning bagel. It could be the prospect of our own wheels, or just getting away from Hate-Ashbury, but he's on his toes and ready for action. Upon entering the airport we're confronted by a line for hire-car pick-up that looks like it will take hours to clear. I'm a little anxious that my online booking didn't go through; it seemed so easy – surely *too* easy? I don't even remember confirming the booking; it was just a couple of clicks and some digits. The process designed to alleviate buyer anxiety is having the opposite effect on me, and not for the first time do I feel out of sync with the world.

I tell Jimmy to get himself a cup of tea and chill in the lounge area with the bags while I wait in the line and read, shuffle forward, read, repeat. It's the only way I can contain the irrational anxiety and be left alone with an engrossing passage about Kerouac's inability to handle literary fame. But suddenly I'm at the front of the queue, being greeted by Aaron from Budget. He's got a big smile and is confidently processing my booking, which he tells me all went fine. No nasty surprises. No hidden costs. No extra insurances or unforeseen taxes. There's excitement. There's hope. There's banter with Aaron about Bates Motel and seeing whales from the coast road.

'Here's the key, Level 3, C1,' says Aaron.

'Auto?' I ask.

'Auto.'

'What colour?'

'White.'

'No drop-off fee at the other end?'

'Nope.'

'That's it?'

'That's it.'

I can't believe it was this easy. We're morons. Fuck the silver dog; we should have done this weeks ago. I thank Aaron and find Jimmy moulded into a lounge chair nearby. I wave the keys in his face, suddenly cocksure, and we head out to Level 3. Amid tense drivers blasting their horns and scrapping over car spaces, we see our brand new, snow white, Ford Mustang coupe. Best five hundred bucks I ever spent. I think of Sal in Mexico: 'Suddenly I heard the dogs barking furiously across the dark, and then I heard the faint clip-clop of a horse's hooves ... Then I saw an apparition: a wild horse, white as a ghost, came trotting down the road directly toward Dean. Behind him the dogs yammered and contended.' But this was no myth or ghost, no spirit. It was no dream; it was our car, our wild horse. We would soon be on the road, no longer beholden to rigid railroad tracks and bus routes.

One turn of the key and we went from shit breakfast and airport queues to Steve McQueen tearing out of San Francisco in *Bullitt*. This beat driving a stolen Buick across Nebraska any day of the week. We manage to hook one of our iGadgets up to the car's sound system, a standard feature it seems, a generation away from cassette decks and scratchy recordings of radio-played songs. The Doors' *L.A. Woman* blasts out as we hurtle through the outskirts of San Francisco toward the Californian coast.

In the car, Jimmy and I find a new and rejuvenated camaraderie, the actual car-driving part of the road trip delivering as only it can. We drive the coast road through Big Sur, taking curves and bridges and tunnels past terrain where Kerouac hit rock bottom. The author of *Go*, considered by many to be the first Beat novel, and contemporary of Kerouac's, John Clellon Holmes, thought Kerouac drank so much not in rejection of conventional values but because he was old-fashioned by nature, and he saw traditional ties breaking down around him. If so, why then didn't everyone with an old-fashioned nature who saw traditional ties breaking down drink themselves to death? From my experience and the hundreds of alcoholics I've heard tell their stories, Kerouac drank like an alcoholic because he was an alcoholic. That's it, that's why alcoholics drink that way. Not for any other reason than that's what they are, as much as others would like to explain it away.

The end of Kerouac's alcoholic solitary delusion hit him hard when he was holed up in the cabin in Big Sur in the early

60s. He'd left Denver and San Francisco for isolation here but was not attending to his real problem: himself. He wrote in 1961, 'the last poor holy fool ... a special solitary angel sent down as a messenger from Heaven to tell everybody or show everybody by example that their peeking society was actually the Satanic Society and they were all on the wrong track'. You can tell when an alcoholic is really losing it: the self-centred grandiosity of someone thinking only of themselves and spending time in isolation, so every thought that goes through their head is correct. There's no one else around to grab them by the scruff off the neck and pull them back into reality.

For a long time when I was drinking, I didn't suspect a thing. In my mind, everyone else was wrong and my way was the only way to do things. Kerouac believed his own myth, that he was telling a messy truth. He didn't realise he was shackled by the bondage of self, never to break free, only to drink himself to death in the confines of his own disease. In an interview in 1986, Holmes talks about Kerouac again. 'He was maddening sometimes ... he misunderstood things, he saw conspiracies where there weren't any ... it increased in Jack with his intake of alcohol. Alcohol makes people see conspiracies.' Alcoholism certainly does, thinking clouded by built-up fear and resentment and paranoia.

Kerouac wanted to be associated with beatniks and hippies about as much as Robert A. Heinlein did for writing *Stranger in a Strange Land*. Although, I don't know of either of them being upset with the royalties they got from the beatniks and hippies buying their books. Alcoholics need drinking money. Holed up in Big Sur, drinking and isolating himself, Kerouac's muddled quest to become the American Proust while hating himself and his fans was a long way from any spiritual sensibility engaged in the journeys of *On the Road*. That time had passed for Kerouac but he didn't know how to let it go and move on. 'Whitman's America' was a time that had passed. Melville's time is gone. Twain's, Proust's, gone. You have to get your own time, your own now to live in; you can't retrofit into one that has passed no matter how much you would like to. If you can't live in the now, how can you call yourself free?

•

On the horizon are three structures I can't quite make out; I want them to be warships, American carriers on manoeuvres off the Pacific Coast, just for me, guarding freedom. I'm guessing they're oil platforms or gas wells or something. As I'm gazing over to the horizon, Jimmy takes an abrupt turn off the highway just for the hell of it, but soon starts doubting himself and panicking about which direction we're heading in. We've changed roads but not course – it's in the same direction, just a different road.

'Does this not concern you?'

'Nah.'

'Why not?'

'Why not? The mountains are on the left and the ocean is on the right, same as before. Just keep going this way.'

'You're certain?'

'No.'

'No?'

'Well, yeah.'

'Fuck. Yes or no?'

'Relax, this road will come out somewhere, we're going the right way.'

'I dunno, man.'

'Then why the fuck did you turn off the highway?'

'I don't know. I just turned. Seemed like the thing to do.'

I pause as I consider Jimmy's reasoning. 'Just keep driving,' I say. 'I'm not using sat-nav.'

'Can you look at the map?'

'What do you need the map for if you don't know which way we're going anyway?'

'Yeah, but you know ...'

I make him sweat for a few more minutes, then look at the highway numbers on the map. 'Keep going and then we'll hit the number one again.'

'Straight?'

'South.'

'Fuck, where's south?'

'Straight!'

After a few minutes, Jimmy confesses, 'Navigation isn't my strong point.'

We're soon back on the major highway that Jimmy veered off of earlier, and with the extra lanes and traffic he's switched back to the Jimmy who sits in Starbucks in the morning, full of hope and inspiration. He plants his foot and the Mustang roars past a few cars as he weaves it across lanes. This is his Dean Moriarty moment – as long as he doesn't take the next exit to nowhere.

With the cliffs and bridges and tunnels of Big Sur behind us, the coastal land flattens out as we approach LA. Dotted houses become clusters and we're soon among the white stone structures of Santa Barbara. We pull into a swanky diner for Jimmy's last meal on the road, surrounded by affluent Californians and a world away from the black denim street dwellers of San Francisco (although the people here are strikingly similar to each other in dress and style, especially the women). There are those on the street looking for community and belonging and those in beachside mansions looking for the same thing.

'Different world here,' says Jimmy, looking around.

'Could you live here?'

He looks out of the window. 'Nup.'

We're soon back on the road and deep into LA traffic en route to the airport, reducing the Mustang's speed to a tame crawl. I ask Jimmy for his all-encompassing statement on our nearly three weeks crossing the country on buses, trains, planes and automobiles.

'I found the whole experience …' he pauses, 'confronting.'

'Confronting?'

'Yeah, but in a good way. Meeting Dan was a watershed moment.'

'Did you get the greatest photo of all time?'

'Maybe. I'll have to look through. I should have taken more shots.'

We pull up at the drop-off and Jimmy gets his bags. I give him a hug before he dashes off for the check-in. We were in

LA traffic longer than we anticipated and I've got us too close to the departure time again, but I feel like Jimmy can't wait to get away from me and out of here. At least he got a few photos and white T-shirts, if that's any consolation. Step Seven says 'Humbly asked Him to remove our shortcomings' and days ago I could have asked God to remove my constant judgement of others and take my impatience and intolerance for Jimmy with it. But I didn't.

I drive around to the gas station near the drop-off point and make sure the Mustang is spotless and full of fuel. I'm sad to let it go. I pull in and begin taking my bags out of the back while the attendant leaves me alone with the car one last time. I'm not sure what I'll miss more, Jimmy or the Mustang, but the double whammy has me feeling suddenly melancholy. But I'm proud that, rather than destroy the vehicle like Sal and Dean did their all-American Cadillac, I delivered the car back without a scratch and got Jimmy to the airport on time, a far cry from previous escapades.

'Hey, Lenny!' I hear from behind me.

Ricky 'The Skater' has come to collect me, as promised, right on time. After dropping my bag at his place, we head out on bikes for a tour through the hood to Venice Beach. Ricky is chatting away as we ride the bikes down to the boardwalk and back past the canals that give this place its name. The ocean is flat and calm as the sun sinks below the horizon, and we stop for tacos before heading back down the beach toward his house. Ricky tells me he can take me on a Hollywood tour and show me some sights in the morning, and I'm happy to be the tourist.

In *On the Road*, Sal mentions having scriptwriting aspirations in Hollywood, but they get glossed over once he is in town and he leaves again for the east coast soon after arriving in LA to go back to his mother. It's as if as soon as he embarks on something that requires work and responsibility and discipline, be it scriptwriting aspirations or the relationships he longs for, the reality of the situation becomes too much to bear and he makes for an exit. Ironically, when it came to sitting at the typewriter and beating out prose, Kerouac was as focused and disciplined as anyone. He had aspirations – big ones – even if he felt the need to disguise them from time to time.

Kerouac wrote in 1960: 'When I wrote these books, I did it as a "holy duty" and thought my manuscripts would be discovered after I was dead, never dreamed they'd make money.' That's odd, considering he sent all of his manuscripts to publishers. No one who assumes their manuscripts will be discovered after they are dead has an active agent or a working relationship with an editor either. The posthumous 'holy duty' was also overlooked when he wrote in October 1949, aged 27: 'I shall have had a Guggenheim Fellowship and travelled all Europe; shall have had bought a house, perhaps a car; shall have perhaps married; shall have certainly loved several beautiful women in ragged measures; shall have had made many new friends, and met the greats of the world; shall have had decided on later, greater books, and poems; shall have died further; shall have come nearer yet to God; shall have weathered illnesses and toil, and binges, and lost hair, and gained wrinkles.' At 27, he imagined his life would become settled and homey. This imagined success was completely at odds with his ideal written 11 years later and completely at odds with his alcoholic reality.

Where does this stream of fantasy finance come from if not payments from writing novels? Writing is all he wanted to do – that was 'the work'. He was living in a delusion of what he himself wanted to happen. Writing to Cassady in 1949 he says: 'Let's you and I revolutionize American letters and drink Champagne with Hollywood starlets. How much you want to bet I can lead us to this?' Why would he even write these words unless he was betting on his books being published, adored and bought up by the thousands so he could make this lifestyle happen? Perhaps the material success was a cover for what he really yearned for. He wrote in the scroll draft: 'All I wanted and all Neal wanted and all anybody wanted was some kind of penetration into the heart of things where, like in a womb, we could curl up and sleep the ecstatic sleep that Burroughs was experiencing with a good big mainline shot of M. and advertising executives were experiencing with twelve Scotch & Sodas in Stouffers before they made the drunkard's train to Westchester – but without the hangovers.'

This was my experience of going through a twelve-step program: a kind of penetration into the heart of things, without the hangovers. But at the heart of things lay a painful and confronting truth that no scotch and sodas or mainline shots could drown out any more. The truth was that in all the bad relationships and failed enterprises and broken promises in my life, there was one common denominator: me. At the heart of things, *I* was responsible. *I* could own it, or *I* could go back to drinking.

•

Ricky and I spend the next day touring Sal's scriptwriting paradise – the palm-lined streets of Beverly Hills, the walk of fame in front on Mann's Chinese Theatre and some iconic buildings used in the movies – before heading up to the J. Paul Getty Museum. Ricky seems to be enjoying life here, being an old skater and surfer. He's one of the few hosts on this trip who's not an AA member, but being an expat Australian and recent divorcee, he's got a useful perspective, and it's certainly different from when I worked with him at a restaurant 20 years ago. I ask him if he feels any greater freedom since his divorce, and he laughs.

'It's all very new and fresh but nice to be emancipated. I'm living my life now, not trying to please a narcissistic partner,' he says. 'I can choose my inhibitions freely and without obligation.'

'Is it weird being alone again? Or freeing?'

'Free, yeah, for the time being, it seems. I can't say I'm not lonely, but I was lonely before the divorce. I'd rather be free and lonely than married and still lonely.'

Sal and Dean seemed to be constantly trying to get into intimate, committed relationships and then once they were in them, they'd run. One's shortcomings are never so glaringly obvious than when you are in a relationship. And for an alcoholic, if these shortcomings are never dealt with, they make staying in the relationship and remaining sober an impossibility. It must be hell on earth for the partner involved. The unpredictable behaviour, the instability and insecurity and blame. It's no surprise that Bill Wilson's wife, Lois, and the partners of the first AA members found a common bond in their own suffering and began the fellowship of Al-Anon for those affected by alcoholism.

'How long are you in the states for?'

'I've got a couple of weeks but am heading to an AA convention in Atlanta.'

'What happens there?'

'A big spiritual shot in the arm so I keep feeling good about staying off the piss.'

'Can't get that at regular meetings?'

'Yeah, but they can be a bit like going through the motions. Imagine going from open mic night to the Big Day Out.'

'Yeah, okay. So you don't want to miss it, then?'

'Fucking long way to come to miss it.'

The next morning, I experience loneliness myself. Boarding the bus to Las Vegas, I sit next to the window and spread over two seats. Only then does it hit me that Jimmy is gone, and I'm travelling solo. No one next to me; no stopping for white T-shirts or photos of alleyways; no arguments over Starbucks or random changes of direction; no one to accompany to meetings; no one else to blame. It dawns on me that I've never even travelled on my own as a sober person before. And now I'm heading to Las Vegas. What could possibly go wrong?

Chapter Eight

Most of what I know about Las Vegas comes from a few movies and the writing of Hunter S. Thompson. Now *there* was a man who could drink, take drugs and write. And he was way better at all three of those than I ever was. He was a journalist covering recreation of all kinds and he covered it well, high as a kite. And an honest writer too. What else could you experience after a time like his in Vegas besides fear and loathing? He wasn't a sad sack either, he knew how to have fun. Rather than spend all his time on Benzos at the typewriter, he'd take acid and play golf, wagering thousands of dollars on one technicoloured putt.

Thompson is quoted as saying, 'I hate to advocate drugs, alcohol, violence, or insanity to anyone, but they've always worked for me.' I'd go with: 'I encourage anyone to drink and have a good time, unless you're one of those people who can't stop it from ruining their lives – like me.' Kerouac himself disliked it when readers only saw a wild and irresponsible duo tearing through the USA and missed what he considered his 'teachings'. Although, from the point of view of a recovered alcoholic, one could argue Kerouac may have projected onto those readers his dislike for his own inability to separate the wild and irresponsible Jack from the scholarly, literary, dedicated writer Jack. I don't think Thompson gave a shit about any of that. They're playing in different literary leagues. Hell, it's not even the same sport.

The bus rolls east and hot, dry desert air infiltrates the cabin as we approach Barstow. Mobile coverage is patchy but I manage to contact Andy, an AA guy recommended to me by a friend back home, who says he'll meet me a few hours after I arrive. I'm glad I won't be alone for too long. Barstow comes and goes, like a blip in the desert. Fifteen miles out from Las Vegas, billboards begin promising life and excess ahead. One billboard urges us to 'Take Back Vegas!' But from whom is not clear. Another advertises *Puppetry of the Penis*, a phenomenon from back home. I thought the creator David 'Friendly' Friend had called it a day after gaining financial and career freedom by manipulating his genitals into unusual and improbable figures. Maybe it's a franchise. Maybe they're the ones who took Vegas, the guys who can make shapes with their parts.

I'm hit by the heat, dust and desolation when I step off the bus. 'Where is everything?' I ask a security guard.

'Down and to the left,' she tells me.

What a great idea – 'everything' is just down there to the left.

Following her directions I enter a large mall with casinos tacked onto the sides. There are bars and buskers and people flying overhead on trapeze-like amusement rides. It's not quite what I remember from movie scenes. I sit outside a Mexican joint for lunch, aiming to take it all in, when I hear a familiar conversation.

'You have the power to stop drinking.'

'No, I don't.'

'Yes, you do.'

It's coming from the table opposite me where a tall and painfully thin drag queen drunkenly weeps, consoled by her camp, overweight and moustachioed rescuer. A Ru Paul and a modern Sir Lancelot. The classic conversation to save the drunk. 'Get an education' is quickly followed with 'Get a job'.

I remember when drinking was the obstacle between me and getting an education or a job; they were never the antidote to drinking.

Lancelot is on the phone to someone. 'Yes, he's right here. He's drunk, he lost his phone last night.' Their voices rise as Lancelot tells Ru to, basically, change. Not like there's not enough on Ru's plate without walking a tightrope between genders in a society that still needs them to be, like so many things, black and white. Lancelot is well-meaning, but even if you can tell an alcoholic something, you can't tell them much. This conversation must be happening all over the world, all the time. An alcoholic, right in the middle of it, with someone who cares desperately trying to convince them to be different. But getting a job doesn't fix alcoholism, it only fixes unemployment, and there are a lot of drunk college graduates. The only solution that worked for me was a spiritual one. I wonder what will work for this poor soul.

The first place I sat down in Las Vegas since getting off the bus is next to an alcoholic and someone trying to save them by telling them how to change their external circumstances. Maybe it sounds more logical to re-arrange the board than alter the way you play. Maybe I'm being given a reminder of what it's like to be in the thick of it so I don't forget I need to check in with other sober people in a city like this. (I didn't realise until later I hadn't even made it to the Strip yet.)

I walk up and down the Fremont Street enclave thinking I'm well past enjoying this kind of thing. It feels like an atrium shopping arcade with gambling and strippers. Actually, that's exactly what it is. A drunk guy sitting on a plastic stool at an outdoor bar fist pumps the air, yelling, 'We're in Vegas!' and promptly falls on his face. A stringy Bojangles-style busker is whipping some bystanders into a frenzy with horrible top-20 muzak. This isn't the Vegas I know and appreciate, the version that lives in the imagination of the world. That place is for real excess, not this shit. That Vegas is about hotel rooms full of coke and chips stacked in pyramids that would make a Pharoah weep; betting the farm on the next card, with a crowd of strangers willing it to be the ace you need, just so one of you can win; taking the woman who has sidled up next to you back to the hotel room full of coke 'cos you're a winner, baby. Even the hangovers are fun in Vegas, just like in the movies. You're supposed to be reckless here, to lose your friends to drug dealers, find stolen wild animals in your hotel bathroom, and hurtle through the Nevada desert, throwing your responsibility out the window. But I did all that shit years ago, without the international cred of the Vegas strip to glamorise it. No stacks of chips. Bad brown bikie speed instead of coke. Ugh. My greatest win would have been finding half a pack of cigarettes hiding under the couch when I woke up from sleeping on the floor.

I've still got the poker tables here though, where sober clarity makes for a profitable asset. I've got to get away from the sideshows and get to an actual table with cards and chips, and players with the desperation of drowning men, playing like the pot is one million dollars and they're down to their last five bucks. I Google 'decent places to play poker in Las Vegas' and find a review for a mission-brown dive called The Stratosphere. From the description, it sounds like they found the architect who designed my old high-school campus and flew him over to Nevada to do it all again – but he made this one a little less inspiring.

I imagine Kerouac and Cassady having a swell time in this place, and it should have been the Rome that all the roads in *On the Road* lead to. But they didn't visit this town; it wasn't on their radar when it was springing up out of the desert and by the time it was a hedonistic hotbed, Kerouac had descended into his alcoholic isolation, far away from the good times of the *On the Road* journeys from New York to Denver and San Francisco. It's easy to visualise though: Cassady on a hot streak as he hits 21 again and again, Kerouac all morose as he loses his last chip, only to be recognised as an underachieving genius by a wealthy widower who takes him up to her hotel room with a fifth of bourbon. Writes itself really.

I sit at the only table with more than two players. The magnificent dealer, a burnt-out hybrid of Phil Donahue and ET, doesn't even try to subdue the loudmouth at the end of the table who's got a stack of chips to match his bluster. As far as they know, I'm some guy from Detroit with a cheap Tigers cap. I win an early hand before folding a few. The banter is going thick and fast between the loudmouth and another player opposite me, just to the right of Phil Donahue, whose deft card handling is years younger than the greying, tobacco-stained rug shielding his head from the downlights. I keep limping in on shit pocket cards when the turn has some royalty and the loudmouth picks up on it. 'He's just stringing us along,' he declares. These places must be absolute hell for the Gamblers Anonymous crowd. Just the interaction with the other gamblers alone is enough to push buttons.

The American Psychiatric Association classes pathological gambling addiction as a medical disorder. I know a few guys who go to Alcoholics Anonymous and Gamblers Anonymous – double winners – but I don't seem to suffer or get an allergic kick off the first bet like I do the first drink. Gambling addiction sounds horrendous. My friend Bryan, a double winner, tells me that the worst part is that you can only drink and therefore spend so much money before you simply pass out. With gambling, as long as you can get a line of credit, there's no stopping. More loans with more interest, legal or illegal. It can get very ugly very quickly. Underworld debt collectors aren't known for cutting off the thumbs, or slashing the throats, of people who drank all their beer.

I grimace as I realise how transparent my plays must be, but 50 bucks isn't exactly high stakes. I'm just here until I hear from Andy or lose 50 bucks, whichever comes first.

Andy's name lights up on my phone.

'I'm out,' I state confidently to the table, striding away with what's left of my chips and dignity.

Andy pulls into the valet area in his silver Audi. He has a bemused grin as he drags on an e-cigarette. 'Why did you pick *that* place?' he asks.

'Atmosphere,' I reply. 'I'm not much of a gambler.'

Andy's much younger than I'd envisioned and I ask how long he's been sober, partly to get a read on his age. He says 37 years and my head starts to spin.

'Thirty-seven years?'

'I got sober when I was 13.'

It turns out Andy had full-blown alcoholics as parents, and he got on to the booze and drugs as soon as he could. But he also knew the future damage it could do and what he was in for – he was surrounded by it – and that it didn't have to be that way, all thanks to the example of his mother getting sober. More incredible though is that after being introduced to the rooms aged 13, he stayed. All the temptation shoved in your face here seems like the obvious trap, but it's not. When you wash up in a place like Vegas, that's when you join AA in the first place and stop. After a few years, when you've got your shit together, your mind starts telling you, 'You know, maybe it wasn't that bad. Maybe now you could have one or two drinks? Like a normal person.' If you listen to that and start thinking you have got yourself sober (conveniently forgetting all the phone calls, desperate discussions and banging and crashing that got you into the rooms in the first place) you're in real danger. I never had one or two drinks. One or two drinks doesn't get you pissed.

Andy's place is a little way out of town, and comes with a small guest house – he tells me it's mine for as long as I want. He shows me how to work the coffee machine and says he's going to a meeting later if I want to join him. That's sober hospitality – coffee and a meeting. A little different from *On the Road*: 'He went right out and bought a pint of whiskey to host me proper,' Sal says of another man's hospitality. 'I tried to pay part of it, but he said no.' At least the sentiment is the same, drunk or sober.

I find it incredible that Andy's mother got him to go to AA aged 13, and I wonder if it was that incentive that drove his mother there. Gabrielle Ange L'Esesque Kerouac, Jack's mother, outlived her husband and her three children. She shared her son's taste for alcohol and was resentful toward any woman who got close to Jack. Her small wages earned in a shoe factory meant they were frequently moving from one house to another, although each house allowed Jack somewhere to stay and write full time after coming back from another jaunt on the road, freeing him up for prolific writing periods.

Their relationship sounds like the stuff of nightmares. Allen Ginsberg talked about Jack's mother, recalling an incident when she said that Hitler should have finished off the Jews. According to Ginsberg, '[Jack] said to her, "You dirty cunt, why did you say that?" and she replied, "You fucking prick, you heard me say that before." And then began an argument of such violence and filth I had never heard in any household in my life. I was actually shocked.' Alcoholic parents and children are commonplace, but not all of them are like these two. Still, not all of them are like Andy and his mother either, both still sober, alive and happily communicating.

We head to Andy's home group, a meeting they call 'Pulp Fiction'. I meet Andy's sponsor, Joe, a lithe older chap with a kind smile, with that relaxed look like Dan had back in Denver. In the meeting, people talk about losing parents and living one day at a time. The guy in the chair tonight, Colin, gives a hilarious summary at the end of the meeting with a line or two about every speaker. Andy tells me later that Colin's son overdosed on heroin two weeks earlier, after a lengthy battle with addiction. And here Colin is, opening up the place so other alcoholics, including out-of-towners like me, have a meeting to attend. Regular people being charitable is one thing, but a self-centred alcoholic, whose son just died of an overdose, being unselfish like that and turning up for everyone else, that's really something else.

Afterward, Andy takes me on a guided tour of the Strip. The hotel casinos are outlandish. Forty-two million visitors per year, he tells me, and more hotel rooms than any other city in the world. A beam of light from the Luxor casino shoots straight up into the night sky, so bright that apparently it can be seen from space. Caesar's Palace, the Flamingo, all the names are lined up here. Andy tells me Vegas has been good to him. House, cars, business, AA. I've never heard anyone talk about Las Vegas as a place to enjoy a sober life before.

Over a burger, I ask Andy what freedom means to him, and I'm especially keen to hear his answer since nearly three-quarters of his life has been sober.

'I had a think about this when you told me what you were writing,' he says. 'The more I thought about it, the more I realise my thoughts on freedom have changed a lot over the 37 years I've been living a twelve-step-oriented life.

'When I was a kid, freedom was really defined by coming and going as I pleased, with full rights to the refrigerator, with no questions asked. That was the limit of my understanding. That's all I imagined. When I asked my sponsor, at the ripe age of 17, how to get free, he said to make a commitment. I laughed at him, because I thought commitment and freedom were the exact opposites. "But through making a commitment," he told me, "you will find discipline, and through discipline you will find freedom to be anything you want it to be." And that is what has been guiding me since.'

'All through your life?'

'Well, whenever I have focused and committed to anything in my life, I have experienced more freedom in that specific area then I ever imagined. When I have wanted to be more physically healthy, or let's call it free from extra weight or physical limitations, I have focused on my eating and working out in a disciplined fashion, and gotten exactly what I wanted. When I've wanted financial freedom, I've focused on saving money, balancing expenses and reducing debt. When I've wanted freedom in relationships, it's come from making a conscious commitment to that relationship, articulating it and then demonstrating it with my behaviour. That gives me the freedom to be me, and not need to hide my defects. When I want spiritual freedom, which is still the most rewarding, I stay focused and committed to paying daily attention to that.

'I read, I meditate, I practice conscious self-care and do what makes me personally feel safe and secure. Could be anything. Could be a bubble bath, could be a crime drama on TV, could be staying socially active with healthy people. A lot of the time, it's keeping on with the Twelve Steps. I still add people to my Step Eight list all the time. But if I just do it, make a list of all the people I have harmed and become willing to make amends to them all, I can do that and be free. And as a result, I feel more connected to them, I feel more connected to myself. To God, to life, everything. When I do it, that is.'

'So you've been like this since you were 13?'

'I'm not totally free all the time,' Andy says, smiling. 'But I usually only lose my freedom when I start taking things for granted again. And then I find myself bound to fear, afraid of losing what I already have, or not getting what I want. But all it takes to relieve myself of that fear is recommitting to what I want.'

'That's it?'

'That's it. It's not complicated, I just make it complicated. Know what I mean?'

Absolutely, I know what he means.

'So I'm just going to go to that Atlanta convention,' he says. 'If I go I might get a reminder what it takes to stay free and if I don't go, I might not. But with that many fucking drunks in one place who are sober now, I'll probably get something. Beats being a miserable bastard.' He smiles and puffs on his e-cigarette. If there's a common binding thread of alcoholics, it's making the simple complicated.

•

In Memphis, I get dropped at an old back-street mansion that's been decked out as a guest house called Bo Dudley. I find the key as instructed and inside the place is lined with fairy lights and welcome messages on the door of each room along with the guests' names and where they're from. There are some sweet old blues on a turntable and the AC is humming away, keeping the hot, humid night air at bay – and no one else is here. I drop my bags and head out for a walk around Memphis' back roads to find a late-night eatery. People open doors for me, smile, give friendly advice and directions and make me feel pretty damn welcome. Maybe it's the Detroit cap. Maybe it's the Australian accent. Maybe they're just good people. I come across a smoke-filled grill joint that serves catfish and fried shrimp with grits and fill up before heading back to the guest house for the night. When I arrive, the lights are still on and the music is still playing – a different album – but no one else seems to be around.

Whoever wasn't around the previous night isn't around in the morning either, but they've managed to sneak in and prepare coffee, leaving some banana bread with a note for the guests to help themselves. I find a rocking chair on the front porch and sip the coffee, trying not to think too much. Call it morning meditation.

I'm still a tourist and wondering what a tourist would do in Memphis. The answer is, of course, to visit Graceland.

The white gates aren't far away and once in, I join the guided tour complete with a headphone voiceover with the dulcet tones of John Stamos. Worth every penny. I can't believe the kitsch of this place. The glasswork, the carpet on the walls and ceilings, the purpose-built rooms, the whole shrine dedicated to the King, the private jet. What a lifestyle. There's even that tracksuit with the white towel folded around its collar like a cravat hanging up in the jet's closet. This thing is bigger and plusher than my whole flat back in Melbourne. So rich and so famous but so not free. Tied to performance, under pressure, wrapped up in ego, hooked on prescription drugs, Elvis was dead at 42.

I leave Graceland impressed but a little sad, and head off in the wrong direction until I have no fucking idea where I am. I took so many photos that my phone's battery is dead so I can't even look up a map. I am old-school lost. I walk down to an intersection with a boarded-up store and overgrown sidewalk where it looks like a bus might stop. Sure enough, a bus pulls up and the doors open to reveal a short-haired woman with enormous hoop earrings behind the wheel. I wave a five-dollar bill hopefully.

'Y'all can't use that. And you don't get no change,' she tells me.

'It's all I've got.'

'You need change,' she says.

'Let the boy on the bus!' I hear from down the back.

'C'mon, jus' let 'im on the goddamn bus!' says another voice.

I get on and the driver gives me a dismissive look but shuts the door behind me.

I take a seat among a bunch of guys who are all talking like they know each other, and thank them for calling out on my behalf. I get a 'Y'all ain't from around here are ya?' straight out of central scriptwriting.

'And it ain't Detroit where y'all from neither,' says another.

I tell these guys I'm on my way to Atlanta and came over to get material for a book. One of them asks me for a pen and I hand it over. He writes his name and number in my book and says, 'If y'all want to know about where to go on Beale Street or whatever, just give me a call.'

Off the bus and following the passengers' directions, I find Beale Street. It's mobbed with revellers. I walk the length of the street, down toward a massive river I can see at the other end. A passer-by confirms it's the Mississippi, after looking me up and down like I was asking a trick question. The river is moving fast, a gurgling torrent dragging logs, barrels, anything that floats, down its course. I feel compelled to commune with the river, to rinse my hands in the water, like some pagan ablution. Then I sit for a while, perfectly at peace. Afterward, at a nearby café, a bright-eyed kid named Robbie tells me that some 20 years ago, Jeff Buckley waded into the river from exactly the point where I was sitting. I remember the album, *Grace,* and reading about Buckley drowning. I would have been 19 at the time, only a few years younger than Robbie.

Beale is an old street, an institution, famous worldwide for its live music and buzz. I can see how I might have landed here many years ago and become a cynical local alcoholic in a matter of weeks if I'd found a way to financially support myself. There's also a reasonable chance I would have thought swimming in the Mississippi was a good idea.

At the end of Beale Street I stop to look through a little photographic print museum, which has stacks of images depicting the 1960s Civil Rights era. I don't have enough time to visit the National Civil Rights Museum itself – it's closed for today and I'm leaving tonight. The irony isn't lost on me that for all my want to experience American freedom, I miss the museum but manage to spend hours gaping at the palatial kitsch of a white guy's fortune made off the back of popularising black music for a white audience.

When I get back to the guest house, I clean up a bit and reorganise all my gear for the overnight bus, but never meet the person who's been putting on the records, and making fresh coffee and banana bread. I don't even have an image of the host at Bo Dudley. Must be a ninja. Or maybe a Gideon like Bill Hicks once said.

Uber driver Jimmy swoops up my backpack and plants it inside the car in one deft motion and chats enthusiastically en route to the Greyhound station.

'It's all about the seeds you plant,' he says. 'Put positive out rather than negative makes you a certain kind of person.'

The trip is over in no time and he's carrying my bags into the terminal for me with that same southern hospitality and help I got when I arrived. Now I just have to sit and wait for the 11pm to New Orleans. Tennessee to Louisiana. On the road again.

•

It's the middle of the night and I wake with a start, unfolding myself from a pretzel position. The atmosphere on the bus is thick with agitation and it takes me a while to grasp that we've blown a tyre. With resignation, the driver informs us we'll have to disembark until someone can come and fix the flat.

I remember Sal's return trips to New York on the overnight buses from California, where nothing much happens and even less is written about. It wasn't that long ago that the bus driver himself, a thin, well-spoken man from the Barack Obama mould, might have found himself in trouble with a local lynch mob in a town like this, which happens to be Jackson, Mississippi. Now, though, most people on the bus are black too and just shitty about having to get off.

I realise the driver can't leave the vehicle unattended. While he is taking all the passive-aggressive blame for the flat tyre, everyone else is free to walk to the gas station down the street.

'Do you want anything?'

'Huh?' he says, with the same expression as the guy in Memphis who told me the massive torrent beside us was in fact the Mississippi river.

I return with his order: a Sunkist and Black & Mild – 'ask for it by name' – cigar. He's even more flustered when I refuse to take his money for it. 'I appreciate you,' he says a couple of times.

'No worries,' I say breezily. I'm not cashed up but I can afford to buy this guy a drink. Maybe I just planted a seed of positivity, like Jimmy the Uber driver in Memphis suggested. Trip money lasts when you don't have to buy alcohol or cigarettes.

Sal and Dean get stopped by police in *On the Road* and fined $25, declaring, 'It was just like an invitation to steal to take our trip-money away from us.' They steal plenty from then on: food, fuel, cigarettes. It sounds like the attitude of an alcoholic all right: the self-importance that means the rules for everyone else, like the law, don't really apply – or when they do it's a personal injustice.

I remember a lady named Pat talking at a meeting. She'd just arrived and I asked her how she was going. 'I hate female police,' was her opener – not even a hello. I asked her why and she told me she got pulled over by a female police officer, then fined for driving while talking on a mobile phone. I asked her why she was on the phone and she said because it was her ex-husband calling and he only calls when it's about the kids, so she was compelled to answer it. Even though she knew that talking on a mobile phone while driving is illegal, and dumb, and when you get caught you get fined, and that all mobile phones have voicemail and caller ID so you can check who called and why and call them back – or pull over and answer – she decided, like a terminally unique alcoholic, that the rules didn't apply to her. Therefore she hates female police. I don't know what happened to Pat but she stopped coming to meetings years ago. When you're not willing to be honest with yourself, you can only hear people talk about honesty and responsibility for so long before you get sick of hearing it, and begin to hate the other members for their willingness.

While waiting to board the bus, this sweaty, potbellied hick with bloodshot eyes waddles over and asks me, 'Where y'all from?' I tell him Australia and get this 'whoosh' sound accompanied by a shake of his head. 'Wow, I just can't believe yous is a Australian!' He insists on shaking my hand every time he says it, which is frequently. 'Whoosh!' Even after he takes a piss against the wall and waddles back with his outstretched, sweaty, piss-sprinkled hand to declare his disbelief again. In desperation, I return to the gas station for a bag of ... whatever.

Dean Moriarty says, 'we know time – how to slow it up and walk and dig and just old-fashioned spade kicks, what other kicks are there? We know.' Yeah, maybe when they're stoned out of their mind. Dean can't slow down at all, he's perpetually moving. Stillness scares the shit out of these guys. They don't know time – they fear time. There is no linear progression in *On the Road*, which is perhaps why it's popular with people who have no linear progression in their own lives; but then, upon a second reading in their forties when they didn't die in their twenties and have some kind of direction in their life, it reads like a secret shame of their past for loving *On the Road* in the first place. It is a book of no direction for people with no direction, or people who think it's hip to have no direction. As long as you're in a country that will feed, clothe and shelter you due to all those squares paying all that tax and those unhip farmers producing all that food, then you can ignore time, man, and just be on the road.

When I get back, the potbellied hick has the palms of his hands on his thighs as he stares open-mouthed at the guy jacking up the bus and changing the tyre. The waiting around is getting on my nerves and I pace circles around the car park near a young guy with headphones doing the same thing. The freedom of the road is never quite as appealing as when it's just beyond your reach.

Chapter Nine

I'm trying to unlock the combination key pod and open the door to Hank's place in New Orleans. Even though I've got his permission and the damn combination, I still feel shifty. Over the road, an older woman rocking back and forth on her porch raises her hand with a friendly 'Y'all' that carries across the street. I wave back as a couple of teenagers amble past and say the same thing. It's a perfectly pitched greeting that says, 'Hello and welcome if you're supposed to be here,' and 'We've got your number if you're not.'

Hank's place is a 'shotgun', which means there's no hallway: each room leads to the next through doors on alternating ends of the walls. It feels like the inside of Elvis's private jet. I drop my bags where there's space on the floor and slump face first onto the bed; I fall asleep immediately. A guy called Jean is taking me to a meeting tonight, where I'll also catch up with Hank. It's like a well-oiled machine, this AA network. Well, maybe not exactly 'well-oiled'. But there's a surplus of people wanting to help others, and they're all, these days, able to get shit done.

When I wake, I head to the French Quarter, and am struck by houses going from orange to purple to white to blue and yellow, beads hanging and flags draped over balconies or sticking out from poles. American flags, French flags and New Orleans flags with their fleur-de-lis. A girl cycles past, pedalling with bare feet and wearing a little white dress, looking like she doesn't have a care in the world. That feeling is in the air here. Bars and cafés look like the adjoining houses, just with a sign or a rainbow flag to make it known it's something else. I walk for an hour before the terraces of what must be the French Quarter appear.

'Hey, Lenny,' I hear from across the street. There's a black pickup with the window down and a smiling bearded fella is beckoning me over. Jean has spotted the Detroit Tigers cap.

'You hungry?' he asks, as I jump in. 'Have you had a po' boy yet?'

'What's a po' boy?'

'I'll show you.' He swings the truck across the road. 'Fuck yeah,' he says with a big grin. 'Yeah!'

Jean asks me about travelling in the US and why I'm in New Orleans 'en route to goddamn Atlanta'. I just wanted to follow the Mississippi south, I tell him, and to exercise my own freedom to do so.

We get to the Parkway and Jean is pretty pumped about introducing me to the mythical and mystical po' boy of New Orleans. I'm tasting fried shrimp in a bread roll and, not for the first time, I feel like I'm missing something.

'The meeting we're going to tonight is called "Neckbreakers"', Jean says. 'You know, after that part in the Big Book about breaking your neck to help another alcoholic?'

I can't remember that bit at all.

'It's a good meeting, two speakers for about 10 minutes each,' he tells me. 'Tonight, one is some woman from out of town, I don't know, never met her. You're the other one.'

When we arrive, there are two chairs at the front of the room and I meet the other speaker, who goes first. This might sound daunting, the idea of revealing your innermost fears and failings to a room full of strangers without notice, but once you've done it a couple of times, it comes naturally. You can't really go wrong, as long as you're talking about your experience of drinking and then getting sober, and as long as you don't bang on for too long. Some meetings have had to put time limits on the talks.

After the meeting, I'm chatting to a couple of locals when a red-headed version of Tom Waits sidles up and introduces himself as Hank, my host.

'So I hear you're a writer?' he says on the ride home. I tell him about the trip and the book and the build-up to Atlanta, and he seems to get where I'm coming from straight away. I ask him about the bookshelf in his home, which looks like a writer's selection.

'It is and I am. You should have seen it before the hurricane. Those books, they're all after.' Hank settled in New Orleans just before Katrina ripped through in 2005. He tells me he was still drinking then. He evacuated and got drunk in Texas while it all happened, then spent some time drunk in Europe before going to meetings there and coming back to New Orleans. Seven years sober, same as me.

He reminds me of Bull Lee from *On the Road*, the older writer from New Orleans who gives Sal and Dean shelter for a while. Except Hank's not smacked out of his mind and brandishing a pistol and, as far as I can tell, he never shot his wife in the head playing William Tell in the backyard. We go and see a band, but I'm feeling dead on my feet and we head back home before long. Hank hands me a copy of John Steinbeck's *Travels with Charley* and another book called *Orangutan* by Colin Broderick.

'That's a good book to read if you're travelling around the States,' says Hank of the Steinbeck title. 'The other one is by an Irish guy who started going to meetings in New York. It's called *Orangutan* because that's his philosophy: in the end we're all just apes throwing shit at each other.' Hank laughs. 'Might be good for your writing though, that angry post-sober point of view.'

The next morning I wake up with an aching head and not enough energy to even get up. Hank has left me a message saying he can give me a road tour later today, and I accept before passing out for a few more hours. I think of Sal laid up in Mexico with dysentery and how his 'good buddy' Dean just leaves him there to rot in pursuit of one of his women back in New York. Even Sal admits, in the last paragraph of Part Four when Dean was about to leave Mexico, 'When I got better I realized what a rat he was, but then I had to understand the impossible complexity of his life, how he had to leave me there, sick, to get on with his wives and woes.'

Sounds more like Sal just got in the way of Dean's next fix, so, like a real addict, Dean left him for it. Poor Sal, addicted to the addict Dean like he's addicted to his mother; sounds like a housewife with a black eye describing her husband: 'He's a good man, he doesn't mean any harm. I just make him angry sometimes.' Or in the case of Sal: 'Okay, old Dean, I'll say nothing.'

I'm sitting on the step at Hank's house when he pulls up and a group of skinny teenagers in white singlets start milling around his black pickup. He introduces me to Quinn and Banger, who call him 'Mr Hank'. A little way down the road, Hank puts on Quinn's hip hop album.

'Quinn's the actual artist. Banger can't really rap but he wants to be, you know, in the mix. He's Banger after "gang banger". Quinn says some good stuff when he's not trying to be all gangsta like Banger.' Hank tells me the kids work on the community farm he set up around the corner on a vacant lot; it's something to do besides all the gang shit. He said the upper and lower Ninth Wards have bad reputations, the lower especially. 'They call this side the riverside and over there, the homicide,' says Hank. We cross a bridge over the Mississippi and Hank says, 'We're in Algiers now.' A couple of streets further and he pulls up outside a white house surrounded by a tall fence. There's a sign on the fence saying William S. Burroughs lived here. Ah, so this is old Bull Lee's 'Southern mansion'. It's not a mansion at all, it's just a white house. I mean, it's a nice enough house, but Sal was heavy on the licence with it. Seems Burroughs made a fair impression on Kerouac.

In the novel, old Bull Lee takes Sal to a Louisiana bookie joint to bet on the horses, where he writes, 'There was one horse called Big Pop that sent me into a temporary trance thinking of my father, who used to play the horses with me.' Sal was just about to mention it before Bull bets on another, then mentions Big Pop, which comes in at 50 to one. 'Damn!' says Bull, 'I should have known better, I've had experience with this before. Oh, when will we ever learn?' When Sal asks what he means, Bull tells him, 'You had a vision, boy, a vision. Only damn fools pay no attention to visions. How do you know your father, who was an old horseplayer, just didn't momentarily communicate to you that Big Pop was going to win the race?' In this city, with its anything-goes reputation, where even the cemeteries are popular tourist attractions, selling Sal the idea of visions seems reasonable, as does elevating Burroughs to the level of an elder mystic.

•

Exploring the Quarter that night, I meet a couple of other Australians, Mark and Lauren, who came to the US mainly for a huge outdoor dance party/drug binge festival near Vegas, and ended up in New Orleans. They don't look or sound like they've had any adverse effects from it either. They're just those kind of people who can spend a weekend on the gear and then go back to life. I was never any good at it before, but I wonder if that changes with time. When I first came into the rooms I was all out of ideas, it was game over. Then over time, I've grown far more capable at handling life and seem to be a different person. If it's about change, why wouldn't the drinking ability change along with it? If I drank to oblivion back then and have changed, would I drink to relaxation now and stop? Or is the off switch permanently broken like I suspected before I even walked in the door of the first meeting?

I have met people over the years who said they were at the mercy of booze, got sober in the rooms, and then went back to drinking in moderation. I've also met many who tried the same thing and their lives have been destroyed. Some don't even know it. I know one old guy, for example, who is the father of a friend of mine and he will tell you he's totally fine.

He even went to AA for three months once and learned why he drank. And he is fine, if 'fine' means you have moved to a regional town and have a permanent seat at the bar, which is also the only place you can comfortably receive visitors, including the only one of your children who is willing to speak to you any more, then proceed to get plastered and render yourself unintelligible on their visit. Yep, sounds totally fine all right.

A close friend of mine recently went back 'out there'. Her life had gotten back on track and her circumstances changed dramatically. She's 10 years older than when she first got sober, so she figured she was going to try drinking again to see if it was just a problem of the time when she first got sober. If I did that here, no one would know. It seems like the ideal place for it, where the population inherently knows sin and vice aren't the same thing and act accordingly, welcoming anyone from out of town to do the same. I should have come here years ago.

Despite my efforts to shut that line of thinking down, because even speculating or entertaining the notion of drinking like a non-alcoholic fucks people up, all of it is playing in my head when I hit upon a busy market square and make eye contact with a woman sitting at a little card table. She beckons me over and I see she is a clairvoyant or tarot card reader or some such bollocks. I take a seat anyway. Denise is a chubby black lady with short dreads, and she seems very official; she dismisses any sign of resistance and tells me to shuffle the cards. I want to show her who's in charge, so I flick the cards end to end like a casino dealer, but I fuck it up entirely and end up timidly mashing them back into a pile and pushing them across the table to her.

Denise deals, looks at the cards, and asks me to look up at the street light.

I can feel her staring at my face, before she says, 'Okay, you can look here now. You are in a good place with your book and your emerging writing career. An older man has faith in you, trust. But you must have faith, especially in yourself.'

I genuinely hadn't said a word to her at this stage, apart from a mumbled apology after not shuffling the cards. I'm thinking, *Do I look like a (wannabe) writer? Have a notebook in my pocket or something?*

'You have patience and need more but your education has trained you. You are writing to help others, being of service, asking nothing in return.

'You sought help to alleviate your vices. You have good parents. Not perfect, but good people. Where you live holds negative energy from people you've moved on from; you need to cleanse the place,' she says. 'Are you moving?'

No, I'm not moving from my place in Melbourne, and it's all getting a bit mumbo jumbo now.

'Your partner at home is learning different things from your mother than what she learns from her own. It was hard for her mother to be everything.'

Shit, Annie *is* visiting my mum and learning how to knit. That is creepy, but captivating. There's no way she could know that unless she'd read my text messages. Now I'm all ears.

'You're neither rich nor poor,' she says. 'You're in the middle, moving money around.'

I just borrowed $200 to help me through the rest of the trip.

She lights up. 'But you've got money coming!'

Woohoo! That'll do me. I don't want to hear any more.

'But you have work to do,' says Denise.

Damn right, I'm heading to Atlanta!

'Most people make an offering at the cemetery, but you're a river person. You need to make an offering to the river.' And with that Denise gives me a list of instructions that, to be honest, sounds like some voodoo shit I've no intention of following up on.

As unnerving as her accurate insight was, I feel satisfied after the encounter, like I've had a good meal. Without thinking about it, I go to a store I'd seen earlier that sells all kinds of weird stuff and get some orange candles and mustard seeds as per Denise's list, plus a small cigar recommended by the shopkeeper, and start for home.

A few doors down from the shop I pass a bar and see Mark and Lauren inside. Mark waves me in and pushes a shot glass toward me. Lauren and another girl I've never met drink theirs. I look from the shot to Mark, to Lauren and the new girl, and I suddenly notice a room full of people having a blast. Then I picture myself wading out into the middle of a big river and not coming back.

'Thanks, mate,' I say, 'but I don't drink.'

'No worries,' says Mark, and downs the shot himself. 'We're going to head over to Bourbon Street if you want to come?' The other two look pretty pissed and Mark's got 8-balls for pupils.

Part of me says yes, but the part that controls my mouth says, 'Thanks, but I'm calling it a night. Have fun though.'

I head out toward Decatur Street and follow it back through the Marigny and Bywater neighbourhood to Hank's house. It's funny how your mind can trick you into thinking you're missing out on something that you've already done, hundreds of times, so much that it nearly destroyed you.

•

I spend the next couple of mornings peeling myself off the mattress with a headache, coughing and spluttering and feeling generally heavy and clogged up. Thank God for Hank's hospitality; I feel like my body has realised I didn't have to go anywhere for a while so it took the opportunity to get as sick as possible after staving it off for a couple of weeks. Maybe it's just smarter than me and has stopped me from heading out for late nights full of energy and bad ideas. When I do get going, I walk through the streets and wards surrounding the quarter during the hottest parts of the day, hoping to sweat the bug out. I get to Saint Louis Cathedral, only to find it closed to visitors. I walk through a bit of Tremé and find myself in Congo Square, the gathering place of French colonial slave rhythms and beats, the spiritual home of jazz. No beats today though; it is dead quiet in Louis Armstrong Park but my imagination creates a racket. I head to a cemetery that's a popular tourist attraction in its own right, but it's closed. Everything is fucking closed.

I circle the perimeter of the cemetery and find a spot to scale the wall, with plenty of headstones to use as step ladders on the way down. A manicured gravel path meanders through a maze of above-ground vaults, some probably home to the slave owners, corrupt business people, middle-class murderers, jealous lovers, writers and alcoholics of New Orleans lore. We all end up in the same place.

When Sal asks Bull Lee what's going to happen to us when we die, Bull Lee says, 'you're just dead, that's all.' But after Sal's 'vision' of the horse Big Pop, Bull Lee flip-flops, saying 'Mankind will someday realize that we are actually in contact with the dead and with the other world, whatever it is; right now we could predict, if we only exerted enough mental will, what is going to happen within the next hundred years and be able to take steps to avoid all kinds of catastrophes.'

Seems like Sal didn't heed the warning or apply it to himself. Maybe Bull Lee was right, and Denise the card reader is in contact with the dead or the other world that he mentioned. Or maybe living in this city at the end of a needle like Lee did, with its mix of slavery and voodoo and God knows what else out on the bayou, just permeates your being and persona and you absorb what's around you. I know people who want AA to work like that: to just sit in a chair and soak in recovery from alcoholism through osmosis and no effort. The cemetery walls get too high, my imagination too vivid, and suddenly I urgently need to get out of the world of the dead and back to living.

When I say AA only works if you work at it, I don't mean that AA is a magic solution; it's just the one that works for me. The 'work' is being prepared to grow up without alcohol or other drugs to numb that pain. Maturation is hard enough for anyone, but near impossible for a real alcoholic once they find a substance to numb the feelings that come with growing up. And then they're on the substance as often as possible, for as long as possible, never maturing, never growing up emotionally. So having hit rock bottom, then managing to write an inventory and share it with someone, the next challenge is Step Nine: 'Made direct amends to such people wherever possible, except when to do so would injure them or others.' Amends isn't about 'sorry'; it's about change. Accepting what's done is done, and being sorry that it happened, sure, but more importantly, actively making sure you don't do it any more.

A while back, during Step Seven, we asked for freedom from the bondage of self. Now we get to take direct action to have that freedom. The alternative is to keep carrying all that shit around, all the mistakes of the past, but that doesn't lead to contentment and freedom, it only leads away from it.

Carolyn Cassady wrote in her memoir *Off the Road*: 'Whatever it is that Neal represented for them, like freedom and fearlessness, Neal was fearless but he wasn't free. Neal wanted to die ... I kept thinking that the imitators never knew and don't know how miserable these men were, they think they were having marvelous times –joy, joy, joy – and they weren't at all.' No, they weren't. But unless you've hit rock bottom and come back up and gone through it, it's difficult to tell from a read of *On the Road* just how unhappy, dissatisfied and far from content these cats might have been in real life. Dean talked about knowing, but there is knowing and then there is experience. Sal Paradise felt there would be great suffering and sacrifice on the way to enlightenment, but he doesn't take any real actions to get it, he just lets things happen to him, a passenger. For an active alcoholic, suffering and sacrifice are a daily occurrence.

Kerouac wrote in a 1951 letter to Neal Cassady, 'I feel the guilt of my brother's death and my father's as well ... only when I die myself will this guilt go away.' If Sal had made a Step Nine amends to his mother and his deceased brother and father he could have lived without this guilt and moved on. It all starts sounding like a bad soap opera. I made amends to my parents and one of my brothers; I made amends to old co-workers and shop owners. I did it in person and with letters. It wasn't much fun, but it helped me get free from a lot of things. Alcoholic guilt, Catholic guilt, whatever your brand, making amends for the mistakes of the past is one hell of a healing medication. But you have to get to Step Nine to do it, which means you have to get to Step One, which means you have to have a desire to stop drinking.

If the drinking is seemingly fuelling your successful writing career and there are people around willing to prop you up and give you somewhere to live while you do it, no matter what kind of an intolerable arsehole you become, then yeah, why would you desire stopping? Except of course if you're still as miserable with recognition as you were with obscurity, like Kerouac was.

In the Big Book, right after the part about making amends and how to do it, it says, 'If we are painstaking about this stage of our development, we will be amazed before we are halfway through.' It lists what they commonly refer to as 'The Twelve Promises'. A lot of meetings read these out at the end, maybe as an enticement for disillusioned alcoholics to keep coming back. This is how they are laid out:

> *We are going to know a new freedom and a new happiness; We will not regret the past, nor wish to shut the door on it; We will comprehend the word serenity and we will know peace; No matter how far down the scale we have gone, we will see how our experience can benefit others; That feeling of uselessness and self-pity will disappear; We will lose interest in selfish things and gain interest in our fellows; Self-seeking will slip away; Our whole attitude and outlook upon life will change; Fear of people and of economic insecurity will leave us; We will intuitively know how to handle situations which used to baffle us; We will suddenly realize that God is doing for us what we could not do for ourselves.*
>
> *Are these extravagant promises? We think not. They are being fulfilled among us. Sometimes quickly, sometimes slowly. They will always materialize if we work for them.*

Who wouldn't want some of this, alcoholic or not? I declare I have personally experienced and still experience some of these highs. But the kicker is the very last line: they only happen if we work for them. It's like deciding to try a new gym called

Exercisers Anonymous after other methods haven't gotten you fit or healthy. There are trainers who will show you what to do, how to use the equipment, provide advice and so on. There are people exercising at different levels and you can learn from them all if you want. But when it comes down to it, it's not going to benefit you unless you exercise when you don't actually feel like exercising. If you decide you don't want to exercise, you can't really say, 'That gym is bullshit. It doesn't work.'

Admiring the river on my way back from the cemetery, I remember Denise's instructions and the fact that I've got the ingredients to 'shape my future' right here in my bag. I have an image of smoking a pipe in a sweaty conical tent by the river bank with an old, leathery Native American who has tied-back silver hair and a flannel shirt tucked into a big round belt buckle, chuckling at me from beneath his sunglasses. I think I'll just find a spot where I won't fall in if I overbalance trying to underarm the items into the water.

The music and chatter around Frenchman Street spills into the night as I walk past and around a busy bar to stairs leading to the river's edge. As Denise suggested, I write the names of the people involved in writing this book on a dollar bill. I find a flat piece of wood that works like a tray, and place the lit orange candle on top. I'm sure passers-by are staring at me like I'm an idiot as I pour the mustard seeds around the top of the candle and, as they start to burn, gently nudge the timber tray across the top of the water.

It's then I realise I'm totally alone. I walk back up the bank to a bench and just sit still for a moment. I find the cigar in my bag and light it up, hoping it might clear my lungs out, or at least dislodge what's in there when I cough. There's a warm breeze coming from down river and the lights on the nearby bridge to Algiers are twinkling through the dark.

•

Hank has let me stay in his place for as long as I want, and all he's asked in return is that I fill in for him at a meeting specifically for military veterans in Kenner. The day I'm due to leave for Alabama, two guys from an organisation called Gateway collect me from Hank's place for the meeting. Their names are Mark and Pete, and they seem jumpy.

'Dude, you're staying here?'

'Yeah. Why?'

'This is *not* on the tourist map; we used to come here to score heroin. A guy just got shot around the corner from here!'

It never occurred to me to feel afraid here. People just wave when they pass and say, 'How y'all doin?' It's probably as safe here as you are smart, like Madison from Detroit said.

Mark and Pete relax a little as we hit the road, telling jokes between bickering over cigarettes for the entire drive to Kenner, which feels like it's beyond the outskirts of New Orleans itself. The meeting goes pretty smoothly and the novelty of having an out-of-towner without an American accent goes down well with the regulars. On the way home, Mark is in the middle of telling me about his efforts to get on top of his addictions when Pete alerts him to the fact that he's taken a wrong turn. They start doing the same nervous looking around again, on guard and tense, but relax when they find somewhere they recognise and get their bearings. I offer to shout them a burger but they tell me they have to get back to rehab by a certain time. So with the knowledge I'm dining on my own, I get them to drop me off at a barbecue joint a few blocks away from Hank's place in the Bywater.

A couple of guys with lit-up faces come through the restaurant's door, then just stop and look around. One is a round fella with a big bushy beard and a ring through his nose, and the other looks similar, minus the ring through the nose and a few pounds. They look so familiar that, instinctively,

I ask them where they're from. Sure enough, they're from Brunswick in Melbourne. 'Just sinking piss, hanging out in New Orleeeeans,' says one. I'm on the other side of the world trailing drunken hipsters from 60 years ago, and meet modern-day ones from the bordering suburb.

I grab a ginger beer to go and sip it on the way to a levee bank the locals call, I suppose affectionately, 'the end of the world'. Sitting up there as the sun drops behind the rooftops, I imagine New Orleans has been the end of the world for many over the years. If I had come here still drinking, it might well have been for me. A blast from the horn of a barge sidling down the canal behind me snaps me out of my sunset trance and I head down the bank, wishing I could stay here longer but never wanting to leave a place faster in my life.

Chapter Ten

'It's a free country,' says Monika, my Uber driver, as she drops me at the bus station. 'But you have to live in it like it is free, or it won't be free for long.' It's an interesting idea, about the importance of exercising freedom, particularly as I'm heading to Selma, Alabama.

I take a seat on the bus next to a friendly blond kid on the way to Mobile to see his daughter. He's 21, has seen active military service, and is married. When I was that age I was just getting a handle on how to waste the next decade by pissing it up against the wall.

I sleep all the way and wake up as we're pulling into the bus depot in Montgomery, far from the centre of town. Or at least, I hope this isn't the centre of town: there's a three-lane highway bordered by a McDonald's, a Burger King, a KFC, a Popeye's, some other deep-fried seafood place, all with signs that rise into the air to the gods of the deep fryer. Waiting for a connection to Selma, I try to get comfortable in the waiting area with *Travels with Charley*. There are a couple of kids tended by a woman with hair that should have been blonde but ended up green. She's got a tiny waist and an enormous chest and is desperately trying to control the kids. The tiny kids are dressed in baggy denim and oversized white T-shirts and would be adorable if they weren't howling at the top of their lungs with tears streaming down their faces.

An enormous black guy appears out of nowhere and flops onto the two seats next to me. He is agitated as hell, mumbling about getting a ride to the hospital and saying, 'How am I gonna get home?' over and over again. It occurs to me I haven't got anywhere to stay in Selma so I put my book down and start looking for a hotel on my phone. The guy next to me sees the phone and says, 'Hey there, mister, can you help me? Can I make a phone call?'

I sit back, resigned, and hand him the phone. We all just want to get out of here, why not help someone else escape?

Within seconds he's yelling at someone down the line about 'hospital' and 'home'. I decide that I'll look for a meeting instead of a room; someone at the meeting will point me in the right direction. The big man hands me back my phone with a 'Thankya, sir, thankya, sir'. Even though I'm sitting right next to him and he's probably not going to break any records if he ran off, part of me is relieved I got my phone back and in one piece. Underneath all the layers there's still a racist, suburban, white punk lurking down there who hasn't been totally eradicated from my psyche.

A white 'short bus' pulls up just outside the door. The driver, a woman with an Aretha Franklin swagger, enters the depot, calling out, 'Y'all travelling to Selma?'

Y'all, it turns out, is me.

The driver's name is Valerie and she's glad to have a passenger. Within minutes it feels more like a private tour than public transport. Valerie asks what I'm doing on her bus to Selma, so I start telling her about this trip. Valerie tells me we're travelling route 80, the route where the 1965 marches from Montgomery to Selma took place. She tells me she's been called the N-word before and not in a looking-for-street-cred, Tarantino kind of way. I ask her if, in her own mind, she is free and she tells me, 'Yeah, I feel like I am. Obey the laws, do the right thing and then, yeah, it's a free country.' She points out a memorial to Viola Liuzzo as we pass by, a white woman from Michigan who travelled down to join the march from Montgomery to Selma. While ferrying people to Montgomery Airport after the marches had finished, she was shot and killed by four Klansmen.

You can learn a lot on a bus. Ten years before the marches here in 1965 there was a bus in Montgomery where a black woman named Rosa Parks refused to give up her seat for a white passenger. That refusal is often cited as the incident that began the Civil Rights Movement as we know it today. I still remember when my friend Jen told me at breakfast one morning, 'Sometimes there's as much growth in saying no as there is in saying yes.' Jen was talking about spiritual growth and when you're an alcoholic or an addict, saying no means not putting your own life on the line by your own hand. Parks saying no to a white person on a bus in 1955 Montgomery meant actively, knowingly, putting her life at risk: Klansmen from these parts murdered a white woman from out of town at the time of the march to Selma, purely for helping black people say no. A younger woman, Claudette Colvin, had said no and resisted segregation nine months earlier but she was a pregnant teenager and the father of her child was a married man, so she was considered not as good a symbol of the resistance as Parks.

Parks didn't go anywhere special to try to be free. No six years criss-crossing the country getting drunk and screwing and driving all night on amphetamines to prove to everyone she was free. She stayed put, was just plain free, right then, in that moment. The man Rosa said no to, the bus driver James F. Blake, more saw it as someone getting in the way of him doing his job and after calling his supervisor, called the police, who promptly arrested her. Freedom for one can be confronting for another.

It may be a long bow but I'll draw it nonetheless: AA's tenth step is designed for bewildering moments when your first reaction might not have been the most savoury. It goes: 'Continued to take personal inventory and when we were wrong, promptly admitted it.' Not *if*, but *when*. That beautiful promise from Step Nine that says, 'will intuitively know how to handle situations which used to baffle us', doesn't say we will have a lock on being able to deal with every new situation. If that man who asked Rosa Parks to move was in the thick of recovery he might have returned her no with, 'You know, I was wrong, it's not my place to ask you to move because of your colour. Sorry about that,' and continued driving. But not likely. This was the South in the 50s.

Valerie is pretty sure there's a $47 hotel in Selma. Heavy grey clouds loom on the right, while on the left are fluffy fields where Valerie picked cotton as a little girl. We drive over what she assures me is the Edmund Pettus Bridge, but now it's pissing down rain and it's dark and we could be in a car park for all I can tell. As I am the only passenger, Valerie does away with the scheduled stops and instead helps me find the address where there's a meeting set to start. Neither of us can make out the numbers on the buildings, so I take a punt and go for a big church complex.

Valerie takes some convincing that I'll be okay, and I'm touched by her concern. Thanking her warmly, I make a dash for the church block. I don't remember ever seeing rain so heavy, and I practically fall into the only open door I can see. There's activity in a room at the top of some stairs and I ask a guy if there's an AA meeting in this building tonight, but he just shakes his head, says, 'Nope,' and walks off. I turn around and skirt the building to a sheltered area to get out of the rain. Lightning flashes like a strobe light amid whip-cracks of thunder, setting off car alarms down the street. But it's not cold and I'm under shelter. In fact, the heavier it rains, the more attractive this place is as somewhere to lay my head for the night. The sound of the church organ mixes with the thunder, and the result is spectacularly gothic. I get inside my sleeping bag and take in the scene. I wonder how long it would take me to become homeless or how many more steps I'd have to take to *appear* homeless, which is possibly a precursor to being homeless in itself. Then, just as I'm about to admonish myself for acting and thinking like one of those hipster wanker dilettantes in San Francisco, a door I wasn't even aware of suddenly opens, and a squat man in a pink polo shirt comes out, flicking the light off and locking the door behind him.

While he's looking me up and down, I ask, 'Can I camp here tonight?'

'Well, yeah,' he says. 'Don't you have anywhere better to stay?'

I tell him I forgot to book accommodation here and am on my way through to Atlanta and a couple of other things.

He raises his finger and says, 'Let me just make a call.' After a minute or two of talking, he turns the phone onto his chest and says, 'Look, I live just across the street, but I'll stay at my partner's place and you can stay at my house – if you want?'

After fleeting images of ice baths and the basements of LA pawnbrokers fly through my mind, I decide to take this guy up on his offer. His name is Jeff and he plays the church organ. His partner is the local dentist and they live over the road from each other. Jeff says his place is small and I have to share it with two dogs, but if I'm okay with that, I should drop my bags and come over the road to Gary's for dinner.

Man, finding this guy while looking for a meeting at the local church of all places ... it's hard not to feel like something big is looking after me. They told me early in AA not to worry too much about what it is. 'Don't worry about who or what God is,' they say, 'as long as you know that you're not it.' That's the basis for my religious ideal. I'm not it. Neither are you. But there's something behind the scenes doing things beyond my scope. Like gravity, or the earth's magnetic field. I see so many people get hung up on this one – what God is or isn't – and never get past it and miss the part about what God or a 'higher power' could do.

Neal Cassady's religious ideals were a little different to Jack Kerouac's. After Neal's death, Carolyn Cassady stated that 'He didn't believe in a good God. He demanded proof, and to him the proof would be if God were stronger than his own will and his own desires. God could stop him, and then he would believe in him.'

But Dean's need for proof is the great cop-out, the great blame. It's as much God's fault as is the colour of your skin. Jack lamented that his teachings typically got lost in Beat mystique and controversy. Their church, though, is the Church of Self. It's all take and no give. Taking everything from cash and drinks to cars and girls to liberties and advantage of others, Sal and Dean end up with nothing more than what they started their journey with (besides damaged relationships).

Jeff shows me to the house I'll be sharing with a German Shepherd named Elle and a tiny furball of energy called Atticus. Jeff's pride takes over and he says, 'I simply *have* to tidy up.' While this happens, despite my protests, he directs me across the road to Gary's place.

Never mind Bull Lee's place in Algiers, Gary's house is a genuine Southern mansion.

A well-dressed middle-aged man with a bright white smile answers the door. 'Hello, you must be Len,' he says, shaking my hand, before leading me on a tour of the house. Portraits of grandfathers and great-grandfathers and great-great-grandfathers line the walls, interspersed with piles of books on architecture, cooking and travel. Gary tells me that this house has been in his family for generations. 'I hope you don't mind, we're having catfish and okra for dinner. There's plenty of it. Red beans too.'

While we wait for Jeff to clean up, Gary drives me around on a short tour of the town and is unspooling like he's been preparing for my visit for months, rather than just having a scruffy Australian backpacker land on his doorstep. He's regaling me with stories of Abe Lincoln's wife's sister, slavery, cotton, the Civil War, the Civil Rights Movement, you name it. We stop at one building and he pauses. Apparently, underneath this building is an area that was once used for holding slaves. There's a grated trapdoor-style chute similar to those they drop beer kegs through on the footpath outside of pubs back home.

Gary says, 'I don't like the idea that that's what this place was used for – but it happened. It's history.'

Sal goes on about wanting to be a black person in Denver but it stops with the jazz players and down-and-out drunks up there: there's little mention of freedom for the blacks in the South. It's a lot easier to put on the affectations of others as a self-declared subterranean fringe dweller from the dominant class, unlike those who were never welcome to join that class in the first place.

Over dinner, Jeff and Gary tell me more stories about the South, Selma, and their travels. Not once do they even allude to the recent court ruling that legalised marriage equality in the US, which occurred when Jimmy and I were in San Francisco. Later I'll kick myself for not asking but I genuinely didn't even think about it at the time, so swept up was I in their hospitality.

•

Jeff sneaks into his own house the next morning to make fresh coffee and leave peaches, biscuits and a lovely note. To think how close I was to waking up in church grounds! I head out, careful not to let the dogs escape – not as easy as it sounds with Atticus! – and walk around a couple of back streets and away from the town centre, crossing a bridge over the Alabama River where there are monuments to freedom. A walkway leads down to the river; it is cut with timber steps and crushed rock, and meanders through cool ferns and woods by the river's edge. There's a buzzing from two guys trimming back the brush from the edge of the path and I stop to chat to one of them. But before we say anything, he hands me a tiny pamphlet that reads, 'Is there a right way?' and asks me if I know about sin, heaven, hell and Jesus. I just tap out of the conversation and keep moving.

I head to the historic Edmund Pettus Bridge. Coming the opposite way on the other side of the bridge is a young man dressed in little more than rags pushing a shopping cart full of crushed aluminium cans. Walking back over the bridge, I notice the hump in the middle. You can't quite see what's ahead on the other side. I picture a gun-toting lynch mob and redneck sheriff waiting there to open fire. On 7 March, 1965, about five hundred Civil Rights marchers came across this bridge en route from Selma to Montgomery. When they crossed the hump they encountered a wall of state troopers and local militia. Without so much as a conversation, the troopers and militia just beat the shit out of the marchers, hitting them with sticks, firing tear gas and charging at them on horseback. Seventeen marchers were hospitalised, many more injured, in televised scenes that shocked the world. It was a walk straight into a man-made hell.

I take a few photos and get a lady to take a couple of me with the bridge in the background. At a coffee shop close by, an elderly fella with a warm, friendly smile invites me to sit at a high table with him when I head for a low one in the corner. He's Joseph Stoudenmeyer and he saw me coming.

'I was there,' he says.

'You marched over the bridge that day?'

'Got stomped by a horse,' he says proudly.

I've no reason not to believe Joseph and I feel privileged to have made a personal connection to a movement so fundamental to our understanding of freedom. There's not much going on in the town these days, but tourists come and Joe waits for them here. I'd love to stay in this shop and this town for a bit longer, but I've got to hightail it to Atlanta if I'm going to make it in time for the conference.

Leaving Jeff's place with the backpack slung over my shoulders, I wonder why I didn't do something like this years ago. Then I remember that the way I used to drink and live meant I could barely make it out of my local postcode, let alone travel safely out of the country. Thinking about where I could have travelled had I not been drinking my life away, I accidentally walk past the faded Greyhound sign. By the time I realise, I've gone too far and will be too late for the bus! I backtrack in a hurry and there's a short bus just idling there. I was late all right but Valerie told the other driver to expect me, so she waited. People are patient here.

Back at the Montgomery Greyhound terminal, I sit in the waiting area listening to a news report that a man opened fire on two military installations in Tennessee, the state I'd been in less than a week ago. Four Marines died on the spot. A navy sailor, a Marine recruiter, and a police officer were wounded. Seems like in the land of the free, there's never all-out peace.

Chapter Eleven

'We are people who would not ordinarily mix,' as it says in the Big Book. And never have I felt that quite as strongly as I do now, waiting to check-in at my hotel. I recognise two people in the queue, and instantly turn away. One of them had been going around meetings in Melbourne flogging a group tour to the States and I couldn't think of anyone I'd less like to travel with. The other is a recovery elitist who I can't listen to for more than a couple of minutes without feeling like I'm being lectured to by a professor who has never known life outside the education system.

But it feels like the whole of Atlanta, never mind the Hilton Hotel, has been booked out by sober alcoholics, so I'd better get over myself. The best piece of advice I was given when I started going to meetings was, 'you don't have to like anyone – you just have to love everyone'. I rejoin the queue and nod to the professor but my body language conveys that's as far as I'm going.

I check-in and, not for the first time, I'm pleasantly surprised that my booking has actually stuck. My buddy Svenson has come through as promised and I get my key. Svenson, who I met years ago in Australia, has a thing for organising accommodation and travel to events like this for people he barely knows. He told me by email a few weeks ago that he'd booked me in with two Swedes and an American, none of whom I've ever met. I don't care; it's cheap. And if it doesn't work out, I'm sure there's a church complex I can head for with fingers crossed. I get to the room and it's empty apart from three piles of personal belongings and only two beds. Shit. This is not good; I didn't expect a palace but I thought I'd at least have a bed. I lay my sleeping bag on the floor under a window, propping my backpack up in the corner.

Near the lift I bump into a guy I've seen before at a small convention in Australia. Shaved head, tattoos down his arms: Ed from Perth. We consider each other with that mutual recognition you get from meeting hundreds of AA members and hearing them talk about their lowest moments and shameful exploits, before learning what they do for a living or their favourite sports team. It's like an international family reunion where the binding thread between each person is a particular way of flawed thinking and a particular way of coping (i.e. drinking). Plus, each person in this slightly dysfunctional family has probably spent some portion of their life passed out in their own vomit.

Ed's just arrived after his own road trip, although he'd planned guided coach trips months in advance to see the classic tourist spots that I chose to miss. We decide to go and register, braving streets crawling with people wearing blue lanyards and lapels adorned with little badges. It's like walking from stage to stage at a sprawling music festival, fans pointing from confused clusters and turning this way and that with phones against their ears. That group energy is contagious and I'm getting a buzz just from the camaraderie, not discounting the fact that some of these people look totally whacko. One woman picks up on my accent and asks me, 'Do you know where I can get those little Aussie boomerang badges?' and I'm disappointed I can't help her out. I wonder about everyone else's reasons for being here. Ed says he'd be keen to hear different perspectives and tap into the fellowship.

I've organised very little in advance, although I am keen to catch up with my buddy Shane, who moved to the US a couple of years back, and Tim, who has lined up half of the people who've looked after me. I've still never met Tim in person; he's been my angel from afar. I start messaging and quickly get responses. They're here all right, but they're all locked into their particular gigs and it's going to be a bitch to find them. I've got a lunch booked in tomorrow at a steakhouse somewhere in suburban Atlanta organised by my sponsor's sponsor and a bunch of other people I've never met before. I've got a number for a guy named John who can give me a ride there and that's it. I text John a photo so he'll know who to look for and he does the same, saying he'll meet me in the hotel foyer tomorrow morning.

We head for the official opening of the convention at the Georgia Dome, one of the largest indoor stadiums in the world. It's expected to be full. That's one big meeting, and I'm buzzing with excitement at the prospect of experiencing the power of all those positive thinkers gathered under one roof. I remember some of the most effective meetings I've attended, and can't help imagining the benefit I felt from those but multiplied by 50,000!

The crowd is gathering outside the dome. The opening doesn't start for another hour or so but people are already lining up to get good spots. I get a message from Shane saying he's saved me a seat. Inside, vendors are selling snacks and soft drinks like they would if the Atlanta Falcons were playing in the NFL. I find Shane and some others I know from Melbourne, sit down, and marvel at the scene. Fifty thousand excited people congregating for no sport, no music, no booze. Just wall-to-wall alcoholics, and I'm one of them. There must be something special here.

A long Olympics-style flag ceremony soon brings me crashing back to earth with a cringe. There's even a flag for the island of Jersey, for God's sake. Rather than interpreting this as a celebration of the fact that there's AA in all these countries, as is no doubt intended, I begin to see it as a measure of how alcohol itself has ravaged so many cultures and replaced so much spiritual practice and connection (often thanks to European colonists). A few local organising members run through welcomes and formalities but I can't help feeling let down; the ceremony never comes alive for me. The more people cheer this nonsense, the less I want to be a part of it. Totally deflated, I make for the exit early to beat the rush.

Back at the hotel, there's a sticky note in the lift announcing a meeting about to take place in one of the rooms. I make my way up, hoping that this little hotel room meeting will provide a bit of serenity. A boisterous Irish woman flings herself into the lift beside me and starts talking at my face. Two floors up she bustles out, her blue lanyard swinging wildly. It's crazy town here. The meeting, unfortunately, does not provide me with the serenity I'd wished for. A bunch of guys from Kentucky turn it from an AA meeting to a mutual admiration society get-together instead. One man hears I'm from Australia and says, 'Oh, great! Can you get one of those little boomerang badges?'

I decide I'll head to bed before remembering I don't even have a fucking bed.

•

'I nearly stood on you last night,' says a blond guy with a thick Scandinavian accent the next morning. He introduces himself as Kim and his friend as Lars.

'I'm Jack,' says the other guy who's got a bed all to himself.

'Did you go to the young peoples' after-party?' asks Kim.

'Nah, man. I just came back here to get some sleep.'

'I hardly sleep at these things. I get too high on the vibes and the after-parties.'

I don't know if it's just me or an age gap that I'd guess is less than 10 years, but I feel like we're at different conventions.

I head downstairs to meet up with John and go to the meeting at the steakhouse. We drive for about an hour and chat about his regular AA meetings. He talks enthusiastically between spitting into a cup from the wad of chewing tobacco shoved behind his bottom lip. He doesn't know anyone coming to this thing either but he's still keen to hear what the old timers have to say.

The meeting itself starts over lunch, and a selection of speakers share their AA stories and experiences as the food comes out. To me it feels more like a love-in for people in this sponsorship group. I wonder if I'll be doing this too in 20 years' time? Maybe this is how it's meant to turn out – from desperate meetings where I was just trying to stay away from drinking a minute at a time to hanging out with the extended family. I started this journey thinking that maybe I'd become too dependent on the meetings themselves, wondering if I'd ever break free. The network has taken care of me, no doubt. But have I just corralled myself into familiarity and habitual safety to the point that I'm no longer open-minded? Or has it become a neurological habit? Have I lost the zing of being newly sober where every meeting presented revelations like it does for Sal in *On the Road*?

I don't say much to John on the way back and he asks me if I'm all right.

'Yeah, I am. I'm just not sure what I'm doing here.'

He pauses, then says, 'Well, have you asked?'

'Asked who?'

'You been doing any Step Eleven on your travels?'

Step Eleven reads: 'Sought through prayer and meditation to improve our conscious contact with God as we understood Him, praying only for knowledge of His will for us and the power to carry that out.' It's what Dan was doing and what Jimmy picked up before he left, but I'd forgotten about it and just banked on meetings to get me by.

John's phone bursts into life and he takes a call.

'Gotta go pick up the wife from her Al-Anon meeting,' he says. 'Cool if I drop you at my hotel and you walk through to yours?'

He waves and takes off with a screech and I find myself in the deserted hotel lobby, slumped in a lounge chair. There are billowing clouds through the huge glass windows and I ask them what I'm doing here, but they don't part and there's no beam of sunlight or angels' choir. Just hotel guests with blue lanyards coming and going through the revolving door. I've got a message from Shane saying to catch up in the dome later for the main meeting and a missed call from Tim, but I can't get a hold of him. I head out of the hotel and walk to a side venue that's been holding meetings with topics ranging from steps and traditions, to prison and rehab.

In one of them I listen to a kid on guarded day release from a local prison; he's allowed to come to the convention to talk about his experience in Alcoholics Anonymous. He's in for serious drink-driving charges, something I got booked for once – I wasn't caught all the other times. This young guy talks about how two guys from AA came into the prison on Thanksgiving to facilitate a meeting and, more than anything else, he was blown away that they would come and do this during a public holiday. They told him the roster just happened to fall on that day.

This young guy reminded me of DJ, a guy from LA who got sober in jail through AA members coming in to facilitate meetings. DJ said it was a pink donut box carried by the little old lady who came in to run the meeting that first got his attention. Then it was the guys in the yard talking about the AA Big Book who weren't gang affiliated or drinking prison wine any more. For the kid here on day release, the power of example got his attention, but it's the changes he feels inside – his attitudes, his perspectives and his actions – that keeps him interested. This is what he talks about and what resonates most with the room. He's still in jail for now, but he's out of the prison of his own making. It's the opposite of Sal's road journeys – Sal had the freedom to move around the whole country, but never changed inside and stayed stuck in his own head, behind the bars of his alcoholism.

•

There's a bigger crowd outside the Georgia Dome tonight but they're not all here for the AA convention – many are camped out on the lawn in anticipation of the Fourth of July fireworks. I follow Shane's directions, find the same guys from the previous night and take a seat. There are a few opening formalities and remarks by the organising committee and then some announcements about tonight's speakers from around the world, including Ron from Australia. We all look at each other, saying, 'Who the fuck is Ron?' I have flashes of Sir Les Patterson or a ranting radio-host type, a dry-drunk on the edge of madness trying to channel Crocodile Dundee to please the crowd.

A 40-something guy in a suit approaches the lectern in silence.

'My name is Ron and I'm an alcoholic.'

Fifty thousand people respond with 'Hi, Ron!'

He takes a staggered step back from the lectern with a big smile, and the place erupts with laughter. Then he rips into his story. He starts talking about that feeling of hopelessness and coming back from rock bottom with the articulate voice and gesticulating hands of a man running for election, knowing he's winning it.

'As an Indigenous Australian, the abuse of alcohol in my life and culture was one thing, but I didn't know I was using it as my solution until I started coming to meetings of Alcoholics Anonymous. The problem wasn't so much the booze itself. Like I said, that was my solution to the problem of being disconnected from my traditional beliefs, my higher power. They refer to this in the Big Book as the spiritual malady.'

I don't remember ever hearing someone from an Indigenous community talk about the nature of the problem like this. Isn't alcohol a problem put upon him? Surely white colonials made it this way by forcing Christianity on the Indigenous peoples of the world and giving them booze?

'But I can't keep blaming anyone else,' Ron continues, 'and keep drinking and expect it to get better. I've still got the defects of character. I'm still dishonest and selfish and self-seeking and full of fear. Now I've got that intuitive inner voice back, like that sixth sense of my ancestors, guiding me to make those decisions that used to baffle me. The intuitive inner voice that the Big Book talks about in the ninth step.'

I know that inner voice he's talking about. I never heard it either until I got sober. It's the one that's louder than the self-doubt, the one that tells you what action to take and to keep taking action.

'That higher power we're all chasing, it's for everyone, whether you're in the rooms or out. But for people like us, it's up to us to get all our own bullshit out of the way and get that connection. The pride, the big ego, the low self-esteem. We have to write it all down, take an inventory of all that resentment and fear and be honest about it, share it with another alcoholic. See where our mistakes were, not the other person's. We can't keep blaming them and others and think our lives will get better.'

Most people in the dome can't possibly know the carnage that booze has caused in Ron's culture and the mess it has left behind, but it resonates all the same.

He taps his chest with his finger. 'I had to list all the people I harmed, not all the ones I thought had harmed me. The wife, the kids, the boss, the family – I had to be willing to make amends to all of them for my mistakes, not theirs. Directly. Face to face. No excuses.

'Who got drunk and hurt my ex-wife? I did. Who was drunk with his drinking buddies instead of at home spending time with the kids? I was. Amends isn't about sorry. I'm an Indigenous Australian and let me tell you, the word sorry doesn't change what's happened. It's about, "I'm sorry I did those things but I'm not running from the truth about them." I'm here acknowledging my mistakes. I made them from my own selfish motivations, and I'm not going to do them anymore. Sorry is about regretting what happened, but amends, amends is repairing the damage and not doing it again. A good place to start is to ask the people I harmed if there was anything else I might have done that I'm not aware of. Then when the shit hits the fan, when life happens on life's terms and I feel all the fear well up and I make a mistake based on self, I can do this in the moment instead of carrying it away and feeding a resentment or living in that fear. That's freedom, mate.

'Then on a daily basis, through prayer and meditation, or talking and listening, or Step Eleven, or whatever you want to call it, I can grow that conscious contact with that power greater than me, that connection I've got now that I can share with you and everybody else. But I've got to practise these principles in all my affairs. All of them. Not just sitting on my arse in meetings. I have to get out there and get involved in life. How can I practise these principles in all my affairs if I don't have any affairs to practise them in?'

Ron is telling my story back to me like he has an access-all-areas pass into my head, and in a uniquely Australian context I've never even considered before. I don't have to go looking for the freedom somewhere; it's in me, if I can just get myself out of the way. Searching for freedom elsewhere, even by supposedly doing the opposite to Sal and Dean, is just committing the same mistake they did, albeit without the collateral damage.

'So how do I keep that freedom?' Ron says. 'I keep it by giving it away. I know, right? Sounds backward. But all I have to do is carry this message to other alcoholics. Keep it simple. When someone asks me to speak at a meeting, I do. Even if it's 10,000 kilometres away. That's 6000 miles to you lot,' he says with a grin. 'When they ask me, "Ron, how did you get off the booze? How did you get your life back?" I can tell them, "I just did this, mate"', he says, waving his hand over the banner of the Twelve Steps.

'I've got a primary purpose now: to stay sober and help other alcoholics. I'm a good dad these days. I'm a reliable employee. A good son, a trustworthy mate, a faithful husband. But I'm none of those things if I'm not sober in recovery – that's got to come first. I'll lose anything I put in front of that. But if I put that first, I get to have everything else.' Ron shrugs. 'Who wouldn't want that?'

Looking around the inside of the Georgia Dome, it strikes me that every person in here has some kind of belief in a power greater than themselves. What that greater power is doesn't matter, as long as it works for them. No one is more right or wrong than the person sitting next to them. Maybe everybody has a different power they turn to. Maybe they only think it's different, but it's all really the same thing. We just don't know. Though, right now, it seems to be working. There are no fights about it, no arguments about who has the real one or who is chosen. It only matters if it comes between the alcoholic and the next drink. That's all it has to do and it seems to be doing it well.

I've heard people say that religion is for people scared of going to hell, and spirituality is for people who have been to hell and don't want to go back. It sounds about right – the Twelve Steps being a spiritual tool kit. The responsibility for me is whether I keep doing the work to remain one of the recovered ones.

'I started a meeting on the Central Coast in Australia for Indigenous fellas. Come and visit – just look it up in the local meetings book. But if you're all going to come, you better let us know – we might have to put a few extra chairs out.' Ron laughs. 'But you're all welcome. All of ya!' He waves and walks off to thunderous clapping and cheering.

It's like one big collective amends with all these sober alcoholics, and it makes my spirit surge to think that they won't be breaking anything or falling down drunk in the street when they leave here. They're not tying up police or paramedics and won't be bottlenecking the courts with drunken assault or drink-driving charges. There'll be less domestic abuse and most of them are probably going to go to a job on Monday and continue paying their taxes. I'm not saying they're all perfect people – many of them aren't even necessarily good people – but they're my people, and they're everyday people now. They're on a level playing field with all the other everyday people, with their foibles and beliefs and hopes and human failings, camped out on the lawn outside the Georgia Dome, celebrating their independence and freedom.

Chapter Twelve

Back in New York, the day before I head home, I take a ferry that passes the Statue of Liberty, a broken chain lying at her feet. This iconic symbol, known and cherished the world over, might not have been built if more than 120,000 people hadn't chipped in to fund its completion in 1886. Most of the donations were only a dollar or two, sometimes even less. The unveiling of the statue was marked by New York's first ever ticker-tape parade.

Whatever your station in life, the idea of freedom is enticing, even intoxicating. But expecting freedom to come from someone else, somewhere else, can make you do foolish things, whether that's searching relentlessly and losing perspective, or electing demagogues to handle it for you. Perceiving freedom as an object or substance that can be produced on your behalf takes away all the responsibility of the individual to maintain it. Monika in New Orleans told me that you have to live in a free country like it is free, or it won't be free for long. Arlen in Omaha said freedom is in your head and your heart.

Throughout my journey I've learned that externalising freedom creates a sense of entitlement to it. It's like a get-rich-quick scheme or an ad for a plastic piece of crap guaranteeing six-pack abs on late-night TV: why earn it when you can buy it? Freedom, damn it! Give it to me! It's got to be somewhere, it's mine and I want it! Just like Sal and Dean in *On the Road*, we're still looking for freedom out there somewhere, and it's someone else's fault if we're not getting it. But no one could sell instant gratification if there wasn't a market.

My favourite myth from *On the Road* is of the two-week scroll draft. While a draft might have been punched out in a fortnight blitz under the influence of Benzedrine, the finished novel was written and rewritten over a four-year period, and revised after. The scroll draft was produced from the accumulation of notes and journals from Kerouac's road trips, also taken over several years. There was no shortcut to the novel, no matter how many people want to believe there was. As Truman Capote said, 'That isn't writing, it's typing.'

But it's all part of the myth of *On the Road*, and of Kerouac.

The myth about the writer extends to the myth of the novel and the man, and the problem with mythology is that some people will defend it as absolute truth, even if it's to the detriment of themselves and others. Who needs to develop discipline, ritual, or spiritual practice? If Kerouac could produce *On the Road* in a two-week burst and be such a success, then we all can, right? But the novel-writing process was not so simple for Jack, and he didn't find freedom out there on the road: he died a sad alcoholic death. Holding fast to the myth of the easy way out will hold you back from growing up. Understanding that life takes work and responsibility and diligence and discipline, that's a step into adulthood, whatever age you are. It's like what Andy in Vegas said about his outlook as a kid: freedom was defined by coming and going as he pleased. That was the limit of his understanding; that's all he imagined. His worldview was small – the view of a child. Then he grew up, and finding freedom became about focus and commitment: focusing and committing to his career, to his relationships, to what he truly values in his life. When he committed to these things, he experienced more financial independence and, most of all, more spiritual freedom than he had ever imagined.

In New York I walk through Madison Park and down Madison Avenue, heading for 454 W 20th Street. It's near the Highline in Chelsea and has become an apartment building. The gate is open but the front door is locked. This is where Kerouac lived with his wife Edie and allegedly wrote most of *On the Road* in 1957. It took six years for him to get the manuscript published, making Kerouac a 35-year-old boy wonder whose life was far from the one readers imagined. Before he lived with Edie, he lived mostly at his mother's house – broke, lonely, and working away at manuscripts no one wanted to publish. When the book finally came out, the success proved more difficult for him to handle than being an unknown. Kerouac wrote in *Big Sur* about how loathsome he found his fame: 'The "King of the Beatniks" is back in town buying drinks for everyone.' I remember Madison in Detroit telling me that freedom for her is about having full authority over your own life, which sounds fine if you can handle that responsibility. For Kerouac, the last person he needed in charge of his own life was himself. His success and fame didn't lead to freedom – only further misery.

The apartment on 149 W 21st, belonging to Lucien Carr, is gone now too, like so many other landmarks from Sal Paradise's journeys. The freedom of *On the Road*, much like the time in which it took place, was fleeting. It wasn't the movement that mattered so much – that only represented being free from restrictions. The Greyhound drivers I met knew this; Michael and Tom were all for having no restriction on movement; Milton, on the other hand, said that he simply wanted 'to live the way I want to live' – a sentiment that sounds like the kind of freedom Sal and Dean longed for when discussing happy relationships, kids and security, but which they could never arrive at. Sal and Dean's movement across country was never restricted, only their movement into adulthood.

I soon arrive at 7th Ave and 20th where the wraith-like Dean Moriarty was given his last goodbye by a now successful Sal Paradise, who had taken some forward steps in his career. It would be great if this had turned into a long, happy, real life for the character-as-person, but it didn't. After the success of *On the Road*, Kerouac found fame and literary recognition, but his self-esteem never did rise in line with his success. Freedom, therefore, doesn't come from outside material gain: it must be cultivated internally, it must grow.

That's the whole point of a twelve-step program like AA: to go through a practical process of finding a higher power, to clean house and learn to help others to find an ongoing solution to the problem, which for me and Jimmy is a spiritual malady: alcoholism. Booze is just our preferred solution. If alcohol was the problem, everyone who ever drank would become an alcoholic, but they don't. The ones who do are the ones who get that seemingly magical effect from drinking, where it removes all feelings of restlessness, irritability, discontent and fear that are ever-present in sobriety. There's a physical craving for more and there is no off switch. It's similar for drug addicts, problem gamblers, chronic overeaters – anyone with a disease of 'more'. The 'mad ones'. The alcoholics and the addicts. The dingledodies Sal describes in *On the Road*, who danced down the street digging everything with Sal shambling after them, desirous of everything at the same time – burning, burning, burning. But for me, and for many others who struggled with alcoholism, there are no 'fabulous yellow roman candles exploding like spiders across the stars' as in *On the Road.* There's no blue centrelight popping. And no one goes 'Aww!' at the funerals of people who die way before their time.

I was on that road before I drove to that second AA meeting and learned about putting something, anything, between me and the self-destruction of another drink. I left my comfort zone and followed Sal and Dean across the country, and it stayed between me and self-destruction, with and without Jimmy, alone and in the company of 50,000 others. This 'it' is difficult to define; call it a higher power, call it a manifestation of freedom, call it whatever you want. But it's with me wherever I go now and it's freedom from the bondage of self and it's everywhere – as long as you're willing to get off the road for a while and let go of what's not working any more. Then you can resume your travels, in any direction you want. The last Step reads: 'Having had a spiritual awakening as the result of these steps, we tried to carry this message to alcoholics, and to practise these principles in all our affairs.' You have to give it away to keep it, just as Ron said. Do this, and you don't get an old life polished up: you get a brand new one.

You're as free as you want to be when you're travelling on the wagon.

Epilogue

It took me months to start writing when I got back to Melbourne but I found the predictions of Denise, the New Orleans fortune teller, held some weight. She had told me that I was moving money around, but that I had money coming, whatever that meant. After borrowing a few hundred dollars from mates toward the end of the trip and trying to keep my head above water working on a few building sites, I got a call up for a TV game show known for giving away big money just for playing multiple choice trivia.

The day came to go to the studio and record the show, and I was expecting little beyond an enjoyable experience. I had to take a day off from a new job, which was actually only my second day there, but you never know what can happen if you just show up. Woody Allen once said it was 80 per cent of success. So without delusion I waited for my turn to answer a few general knowledge questions, hopefully correctly. It went well – very well in fact. I left with a novelty cheque for $50,000, enough to wipe old credit card debt and leave some for a seemingly adult amount in the savings account.

With this unexpected windfall sitting happily in the bank, I went back to work and stayed there and wrote the majority of this book outside the hours of the everyday grind, missing deadlines and making all of the mistakes a novice writer is explicitly told to avoid.

Jimmy is still taking photographs. At the time of writing, he and all the other AA members we met on our travels are, as far as I know, still sober and still happy about it. It doesn't always work out that way though. Someone I know who got sober about the same time I did is back drinking, even though their partner died from active alcoholism. Another is looking at multiple counts of fraud and serious jail time. Just putting the drink down for a while does not guarantee any immunity from life and life's consequences.

For those people who can have a few drinks, or even put away a lot with no real negative consequences, more power to you. In fact, I'd like to tell you to have one or two for me. I once drank with you and enjoyed your company. But then we parted ways – you all went off and got on with your lives, occasionally blowing off steam on a weekend binge but showing up for life the next day like nothing had happened.

But for those who can't just take it or leave it, and for those in situations where it might be costing you more than money, be careful to see what you're doing for what it really is. If you need to do something about your drinking, make sure you actually *do it*. There's a lot of help out there if you want it.

If the predictions of a clairvoyant continue to come to pass, this may not be my only examination of freedom, change and old literary journeys. While I visited a vast collection of states in the footsteps, or more accurately the tyre treads, of Kerouac, there were many I missed: Florida, Texas, Washington DC, the North Eastern states and the Pacific North West – pretty much all the places John Steinbeck visited with his companion poodle when he ventured around the US in his campervan. It may be fitting to look at freedom and liberty beyond the individual, beyond my own, and examine the idea of a free country: the institutions and structures of the great democracy that binds it together as a whole, against the twelve traditions of AA that keep that benign anarchy from imploding in on itself or getting too big for its boots. I mean, freedom is great for me, but what about the next person? How can I help them get theirs? After all, it's not all about me.

Acknowledgements

First and foremost, I'd like to thank Martin Hughes at Affirm Press for his unwavering support, blind faith and extraordinary patience. Without these, this book would not have happened. Thank you to Keiran Rogers for a steady supply of optimism, Kylie Mason and Cosima McGrath for their excellent editing of the manuscript and Grace Breen for successfully wrestling with publicising an anonymous author. I'd also like to thank Stephanie Bishop-Hall, Ruby Ashby-Orr and the team at Affirm Press for their camaraderie and help over the years.

For those who got me into this mess: thank you to Paul Sutton, Andrew Humphries and Chris Herz for getting me through university and into a position to undertake this project. Thank you to Craig McCleod for creative collaboration and Julian Dolman for tips on overnight travel, aperture and reading material.

Thank you to the BWAP (Bachelor of Writing and Publishing) staff and students at Melbourne's NMIT for their support during and after my studies, in particular Brad Webb, Edwina Preston, Rob Griffiths, Adam Casey, Alice Robinson, Amy Espeseth and Karen Simpson-Nikakis.

A big thanks goes to Damian McLindon and Ben O'Mara for years of setting an example, and to Howard Bolton for solid banter and book recommendations throughout the entire process.

Thanks to Tom Uhl, Zachary George, David Huff, Jack Eggers, Sean Hillis, Tom Needham, Drew Pawlak, Rob Theaker, Gery Anderson, Jeffrey Bennet and Scott Faith for a place to stay and a helping hand.

Thank you to Mum and Dad for a lifetime of quiet encouragement and thank you to my partner Natalie for learning as we go and managing to live with someone working full time while trying to write a book. Looks like we made it.

Finally, a special thank you to all of Bill's friends in The Firm who directly and indirectly contributed to this book. I can't wait to hear all of your opinions on how I should have written it differently and how you would have done it better, at every meeting, from here to eternity. And I wouldn't want it any other way.